General E
Associate E

File on
O'CASEY

Compiled by Nesta Jones

Methuen. London and New York

A Methuen Paperback
First published in 1986 in
simultaneous hardback and paperback editions
by Methuen London Ltd,
11 New Fetter Lane, London EC4P 4EE
and Methuen Inc, 29 West 35th Street,
New York, NY 10001

Copyright in the compilation
© 1986 by Nesta Jones
Copyright in the series format
© 1986 by Methuen London Ltd
Copyright in editorial presentation
© 1986 by Simon Trussler

Phototypeset in Times Roman
by Words & Pictures Ltd,
Thornton Heath, Surrey
Printed in Great Britain

British Library Cataloguing in Publication Data

File on O'Casey—(Writer–Files)
    1. O'Casey, Sean—Criticism and interpretation
    I. Jones, Nesta   II. Series
    822'.912   PR6029.C33Z/

    ISBN 0-413-53650-5 Pbk

*Cover image based on a photo
by Jane Bown*

Contents

General Editor's Introduction 5

1: A Brief Chronology 7

2: The Plays 15

The Shadow of a Gunman 15
Cathleen Listens In 18
Juno and the Paycock 20
Nannie's Night Out 26
The Plough and the Stars 27
The Silver Tassie 34
Within the Gates 41
The End of the Beginning 45
A Pound on Demand 46
The Star Turns Red 48
Purple Dust 52
Red Roses for Me 57
Oak Leaves and Lavender 62
Cock-a-Doodle Dandy 65
Hall of Healing 69
Time to Go 71
Bedtime Story 72
The Bishop's Bonfire 73
The Drums of Father Ned 77
Behind the Green Curtains 79
The Moon Shines on Kylenamoe 80
Figuro in the Night 81

3: Non-Dramatic Writing 82

4: The Writer on His Work 85

5: A Select Bibliography 90
  a: Primary Sources 90
  b: Secondary Sources 92

The theatre is, by its nature, an ephemeral art: yet it is a daunting task to track down the newspaper reviews, or contemporary statements from the writer or his director, which are often all that remain to help us recreate some sense of what a particular production was like. This series is therefore intended to make readily available a selection of the comments that the critics made about the plays of leading modern dramatists at the time of their production – and to trace, too, the course of each writer's own views about his work and his world.

In addition to combining a uniquely convenient source of such elusive *documentation*, the 'Writer–Files' series also assembles the *information* necessary for readers to pursue further their interest in a particular writer or work. Variations in quantity between one writer's output and another, differences in temperament which make some readier than others to talk about their work, and the variety of critical response, all mean that the presentation and balance of material shifts between one volume and another: but we have tried to arrive at a format for the series which will nevertheless enable users of one volume readily to find their way around any other.

Section 1, 'A Brief Chronology', provides a quick conspective overview of each playwright's life and career. *Section 2* deals with the plays themselves, arranged chronologically in the order of their composition: information on first performances, major revivals, and publication is followed by a brief synopsis (for quick reference set in slightly larger, italic type), then by a representative selection of the critical response, and of the dramatist's own comments on the play and its theme.

Section 3 offers concise guidance to each writer's work in non-dramatic forms, while *Section 4*, 'The Writer on His Work', brings together comments from the playwright himself on more general matters of construction, opinion, and artistic development. Finally, *Section 5* provides a bibliographical guide to other primary and secondary sources of further reading, among which full details will be found of works cited elsewhere under short titles, and of collected editions of the plays – but not of individual titles, particulars of which will be found with the other factual data in Section 2.

The 'Writer–Files' hope by striking this kind of

balance between information and a wide range of opinion to offer 'companions' to the study of a wide range of major playwrights in the modern repertoire – not in that dangerous pre-digested fashion which can too readily quench the desire to read the plays themselves, nor so prescriptively as to allow any single line of approach to predominate, but rather to encourage readers to form their own judgements of the plays, to set against the many views here represented.

Sean O'Casey has not been kindly dealt with by the theatre of his native Ireland or his adopted England. His reputation failed to survive the acclaim which greeted his earliest plays, as he himself quickly outgrew their seemingly realistic, semi-autobiographical vein – while the theatre and the critics for which he wrote resolutely preferred the more familiar fare.

Among the fascinations of this volume, therefore, is hearing O'Casey's own voice, steadily and confidently aware of his own stylistic evolution – from heightened naturalism, to a sort of bold Celtic expressionism, to his own highly personal but gregariously generous form of celebratory theatre – in resolute discord with the views of most of his critics. He could not win: while the Catholic right shortsightedly condemned him for an anti-Catholicism which was closer to anti-authoritarianism, the 'progressives' bemoaned what was essentially his truth to his own vision – of a theatre capable of expressing more than modish self-questioning, let alone bourgeois self-satisfaction.

In spite of the continuing championship of his work from some unsuspected transatlantic sources – notably the Broadway critic Brooks Atkinson – and the honourable but unsustained revival of interest in his work at the Mermaid Theatre, London, in the early 'sixties, O'Casey never quite managed to overcome such a handicap of misconception. But his reputation is growing in some unlikely places – notably, in France and central Europe, as the revivals noted in this volume suggest. And hopefully this little collection itself, by helping to identify the 'real' O'Casey amidst the false images fixed upon his plays, will serve in its own way to assist the rediscovery of O'Casey, not simply as the major dramatist of the Irish rebellion, but as one who gave sparkling expression to the continuing, questing, joyous rebellion of the human spirit itself.

Simon Trussler

1880   30 Mar., born John Casey, youngest son of Michael Casey, a clerk, and Susan (*née* Archer). 28 July, baptised in the Protestant faith at St. Mary's Church, Dublin. The large family (five of thirteen children survived) lived at 85 Upper Dorset Street, in the northern part of the city.

1882   Family moved to a smaller house at 9 Innisfallen Parade when his sister Bella left home to train as a teacher.

1885   Developed an eye affliction, from which he was to suffer throughout his life. Attended St. Mary's Infants' School where Bella was principal teacher.

1886   Sept., Michael Casey died, aged 49, leaving little money. Family gradually declined into poverty.

1887   Brothers Tom and Mick enlisted in the army, further reducing family income.

1888   Attended St. Mary's National School.

1889   Reduced circumstances forced another move, to 22 Hawthorne Terrace in St. Barnabas Parish.

1890   Briefly attended St. Barnabas National School; his departure marked the end of his formal education.

1891   Introduced to the theatre by Archie, a keen amateur actor who also took his younger brother to professional productions at the Queen's Theatre.

1894   Started work as a stock boy for a wholesale chandlers.

1895   Chosen by Charles Dalton, an actor-manager friend of Archie's, to play Father Dolan in Boucicault's *The Shaughraun* at the old Mechanics Theatre in Abbey Street (later to become the Abbey Theatre). Tom completed his army service and he and Mick regained their jobs with the GPO.

1897   O'Casey sacked for impertinence; Tom out of work with a severe illness; Archie joined a touring theatre company. Economic pressure forced Susan Casey to move house again, to 18 Abercorn Road, where the family lived in two rooms.

1898   Prepared for Confirmation in the Church of Ireland by the young curate of St. Barnabas, who also obtained a job for O'Casey with a wholesale newsagent. Dismissed after a week for refusing to take off his cap while receiving his pay.

1899   At the outbreak of the Boer War Tom, as a reservist, was called up; Mick and Archie left to support the family.

1900   Rev. Edward Griffin, the rector of St. Barnabas, befriended O'Casey, who taught in the Sunday School for the next three years. Despite Susan O'Casey's opposition, Archie married a Catholic girl and left home.

1902-03   O'Casey began working as a labourer for the Great Northern Railway. Joined the Drumcondra branch of the Gaelic League, learned the Irish language, and gaelicized his name to Sean O'Cathasaigh. Joined the Gaelic Athletic Association and the Irish Republican Brotherhood (IRB). His active involvement in Church affairs continued, particularly over the issue of introducing Irish-speaking clergy.

1905   Recruited Ernest Blythe into the IRB: Blythe was later to become a member of the first Free State Government and Managing Director of the Abbey Theatre.

1907   Joined St. Laurence O'Toole Club and three years later formed the St. Laurence O'Toole Pipers Band with Frank Cahill, a committed Republican and nationalist. 25 May, published his first article, 'Sound the Loud Trumpet', in *The Peasant and Irish Ireland*, which fiercely attacked the educational system and denounced British rule in Ireland. His religious fervour began to lose some of its intensity and formal relationship with the Church ceased.

1909   Jim Larkin founded the Irish Transport and General Workers Union (ITGWU).

1911   Railway strike (the background to *Red Roses for Me*). O'Casey joined Larkin's Union and wrote his first play for an amateur group. Dismissed from his job at the Great Northern Railway due to his criticism of working conditions and his refusal to sign a document undertaking not to join the Union. Unemployment brought considerable hardship to O'Casey and his mother.

1912   O'Casey contributed regularly to the *Irish Worker* (a union newspaper founded by Larkin) and the nationalist periodical *Irish Freedom*. Under the influence of Larkin his commitment to the Labour movement hardened, but his wish to unite the Labour and Nationalist movements to achieve the ideal of an Irish Workers'

Republic met with little sympathy from either the Gaelic League or the IRB. Subsequently he resigned from both organizations as he perceived within them a growing 'middle class nationalism'.

1913 July, became secretary of the Wolfe Tone Committee. Industrial unrest, brewing since the strike in 1911, reached a head when Dublin employers locked-out all members of the ITGWU, and Larkin retaliated by calling for a general strike. This lock-out and its aftermath had a profound effect on O'Casey's political thinking. Sept., Larkin addressed a large demonstration during which police made a baton charge killing two people and wounding several hundreds. Oct., the trade union formed the Irish Citizen Army (ICA) as a defence measure against police brutality. Nov., the Irish Volunteers, a paramilitary nationalist organization, formed. A Strikers' Relief Fund established, with O'Casey as its secretary, but resistance to the lock-out weakened as the winter wore on.

1914 6 Feb., his brother Tom died, aged 44. Mar., O'Casey elected secretary of the reorganized ICA. He drew up the constitution which emphasized its socialist and nationalist basis, but recruitment was slow and hostility continued between the ICA and the Volunteers. The outbreak of the Great War caused a split in the latter: the majority followed the parliamentary leader John Redmond, who pledged support to Britain and the Empire, but a militant minority, heavily infiltrated by the IRB, prepared for revolt against Britain. Countess Markievicz urged the ICA to join the militant wing. O'Casey opposed this, unsuccessfully moved a resolution demanding that she choose between the organizations, and on 17 July resigned from the ICA.

1915 O'Casey's involvement with the lock-out and the ICA led to unemployment. Aug., admitted to St. Vincent's Hospital for an operation on a swollen tubercular gland in his neck. Oct., Larkin left Ireland to raise funds for the ITGWU in America; James Connolly succeeded Larkin as leader of the Labour movement. O'Casey became increasingly disaffected with the ICA as he believed Connolly's policy was taking it further away from its Labour roots.

1916 Published 'The Grand Oul' Dame Britannia', an anti-war ballad. 24-29 Apr., insurrection against the British authorities, known as the Easter Rising, led by the Volunteers and ICA (background to *The Plough and the Stars*). The British quelled the Rising within a week (Irish casualties: about 46 killed and 2,600 wounded, many of them non-combatants) and executed fourteen of the ringleaders, among them Connolly and Padraic Pearse. O'Casey took no active part in the Rising, although he was much affected by it.

1917   Met Maura Keating, his first steady girl-friend, at St. Laurence O'Toole Dramatic Club. Sept., 'Lament for Thomas Ashe' published, a moving tribute to the patriot, also his friend, who died while on hunger strike in Mountjoy Prison.

1918   1 Jan., Bella died, aged 52. Mar.-May, *Songs of the Wren No. 1*, *Songs of the Wren No. 2*, and *More Songs of the Wren* published. 9 Nov., Susan Casey died, aged 81.

1919   'The Story of the Irish Citizen Army' published. Guerilla warfare in Ireland between Irish Republican Army (successor to the Volunteers) and British forces.

1920   Abbey Theatre rejected his first two plays, *The Frost in the Flower* and *The Harvest Festival*. Moved to a tenement at 35 Mountjoy Square where he shared a room with Michael O'Maolain. Royal Irish Constabulary reinforced by the Black and Tans – mostly ex-servicemen recruited in Britain: atrocities, reprisals, ambushes, and midnight raids (background to *The Shadow of a Gunman*). O'Casey worked as a caretaker and also acted as secretary of the Release Jim Larkin Committee, Larkin having been imprisoned in the USA.

1921   Moved to a room at 422 North Circular Road. 6 Dec., Peace Treaty signed, partitioning the country into an independent Irish Free State and the northern Six Counties within the United Kingdom. British troops withdrawn.

1922   Apr., Abbey Theatre rejected *The Seamless Coat of Kathleen* and in Sept. *The Crimson and the Tri-Colour*, but in Nov. the board accepted *On the Run*, retitled *The Shadow of a Gunman*. Changed his name to Sean O'Casey. Civil war broke out in the South between the Free Staters, who supported the Treaty and partition, and the Diehard Republicans who rejected both (background to *Juno and the Paycock*).

1923   12 Apr., *The Shadow of a Gunman* staged at the Abbey Theatre for four performances at the end of the season; author's royalties amounted to £4. But when the theatre opened in Aug. with *Gunman* it played to capacity houses. O'Casey continued to work as a labourer, but became a regular visitor to the Abbey. 1 Oct., *Kathleen Listens In* staged at the Abbey in a triple-bill.

1924   3 Mar., *Juno and the Paycock* staged at the Abbey, but despite its popularity some objected to it on moral grounds and others condemned what they considered an unfavourable depiction of the struggle for independence. On the strength of *Juno*'s success

O'Casey became a full-time writer and joined the Society of Authors and Playwrights. 29 Sept., *Nannie's Night Out* staged at the Abbey.

1925 10 Feb., publication of *Two Plays* (*Juno* and *Gunman*). 16 Nov., London premiere of *Juno and the Paycock* at the Royalty Theatre.

1926 8 Feb., *The Plough and the Stars* staged at the Abbey, but on the fourth night a planned demonstration led to a riot. In a climate of personal and professional hostility, O'Casey decided to leave for London, where he had just been awarded the Hawthorden Literary Prize for *Juno and the Paycock*. Mar., American premiere of *Juno*. Apr., publication of *The Plough and the Stars*. O'Casey met Irish born actress Eileen Carey. 12 May, British premiere of *The Plough and the Stars*. Augustus John painted O'Casey's portrait. July, moved to South Kensington, London.

1927 27 May, British premiere of *The Shadow of a Gunman*. 23 Sept., married Eileen Carey at the Catholic Church of the Most Holy Redeemer, Chelsea. Honeymoon was spent in Howth and Dublin. 27 Nov., American premiere of *The Plough and the Stars*. Growing commitment to international socialism.

1928 Jan., moved to St. John's Wood, London. 17 Mar., sent his new play *The Silver Tassie* to the Abbey. 30 Apr., his son Breon born. On the same day O'Casey received news from Lady Gregory that the Abbey directorate had rejected *The Silver Tassie*, and a public controversy ensued.

1929 11 Oct., *The Silver Tassie* staged at the Apollo Theatre, London, with Act II designed by Augustus John. The first week's receipts broke the box-office records, but the show closed after eight weeks, largely due to the slump brought on by the Wall Street Crash. 24 Oct., American premiere of *The Silver Tassie*.

1930 22 Sept., film of *Juno and the Paycock* released. 10 Nov., copy of the film burned by Irish nationalists in Limerick.

1931 Sept., moved to Chalfont St. Giles, Buckinghamshire.

1932 Refused an invitation by Yeats and Shaw to become a member of the Irish Academy of Letters. Seriously in debt, O'Casey sold half the amateur rights of the Dublin plays to Samuel French for £300.

1933 May, his short story 'I Wanna Woman' censored by the printer of *Time and Tide*. 24 Nov., publication of *Within the Gates*.

1934   7 Feb., *Within the Gates* opened in London. 13 Sept., sailed for New York for American premiere. 16 Oct., publication of *Windfalls*. 22 Oct., *Within the Gates* opened in New York, and ran for 102 performances. 16 Nov., gave the Morris Gray Poetry Talk at Harvard University entitled 'The Old Drama and the New'. 4 Dec., *Windfalls* banned by Irish Censorship of Publications Board. 12 Dec., O'Casey left New York.

1935   11 Jan., second son Niall born. 12 Aug., Irish premiere of *The Silver Tassie* at the Abbey accompanied by protests from the Irish clergy. Sept., O'Casey reconciled with Yeats during a short visit to Dublin.

1936   Jan., Gave a talk to the Shirley Society of St. Catherine's College, Cambridge, entitled 'The Holy Ghost Leaves England', which attacked English attitudes and politics.

1937   8 Feb., *The End of the Beginning* staged at the Abbey. 5 Mar., publication of *The Flying Wasp*. 15 Mar., film of *The Plough and the Stars* released.

1938   Sept., moved to Tingrith, Devon, so that his sons could be educated at Dartington Hall.

1939   3 Mar., publication of *I Knock at the Door*, first volume of autobiography: banned in Ireland. 28 Sept., daughter Shivaun born.

1940   15 Feb., publication of *The Star Turns Red*. June, became a member of the editorial board of *The Daily Worker*. 19 Nov., publication of *Purple Dust*.

1942   17 Feb., publication of *Pictures in the Hallway*, also banned in Ireland. 17 Nov., publication of *Red Roses for Me*.

1943   15 Mar., *Red Roses for Me* staged at the Olympia Theatre, Dublin, first O'Casey play to be staged in Dublin for seventeen years. 16 Dec., *Purple Dust* staged at the People's Theatre, Newcastle-upon-Tyne.

1945   16 Oct., publication of *Drums under the Windows*.

1946   30 Apr., publication of *Oak Leaves and Lavender*. 28 Nov., *Oak Leaves and Lavender* premiered in Sweden.

1947   11 Jan., brother Mick died in Dublin, aged 81. 30 Jan., Jim Larkin died, aged 69. 13 May, English premiere of *Oak Leaves and Lavender*. 16 Dec., Irish Censorship of Publications Board removed ban against *I Knock at the Door* and *Pictures in the Hallway*.

1949   28 Jan., publication of *Inishfallen, Fare Thee Well*.

Received Page One Award of Newspaper Guild of New York for autobiographies. Publication of *Cock-a-Doodle Dandy*. 11 Nov., publication of first two volumes of *Collected Plays*.

1951 17 Jul., publication of last two volumes of *Collected Plays*.

1952 4 July, publication of *Rose and Crown*.

1954 9 June, the O'Casey family moved to St. Marychurch, Devon. 29 Oct., publication of *Sunset and Evening Star*, last volume of autobiography.

1955 28 Feb., *The Bishop's Bonfire* staged at the Gaiety Theatre, Dublin, and published 24 June.

1956 22 Jan., *A Conversation with Sean O'Casey* broadcast by NBC-TV. Feb., prostate operation and further operation to remove a stone in his kidney followed by a severe attack of bronchitis. Mar., publication of *The Green Crow*. 27 Dec., American premiere of *Purple Dust*, which ran for fourteen months. 29 Dec., youngest son, Niall, died of leukemia.

1957 Feb., the Irish Customs Office seized *The Green Crow* and the book was unofficially banned for a year. May, a selection of plays published in Russia. Oct., *The Drums of Father Ned* accepted by the Dublin Tostal Council for performance at the International Theatre Festival the following year. *Bloomsday*, a dramatization of James Joyce's *Ulysses*, also chosen.

1958 Jan., Archbishop of Dublin, Most Rev. Dr. McQuaid, refused to mark the Tostal by an official mass if either of the plays were included in the Festival, and both works were withdrawn. O'Casey banned professional productions of any of his plays in Dublin: not lifted until 1964.

1959 Appeared in conversation with Barry Fitzgerald in a film about the Abbey, *The Cradle of Genius*, released in USA in 1961. Feb., publication of *The Star Turns Red* in China. 9 Mar., *Juno*, musical based on O'Casey's play, opened at the Winter Garden Theatre, New York. 25 Apr., *The Drums of Father Ned* premiered at the Little Theatre, Lafayette, Indiana. 17 Sept., *Cock-a-Doodle Dandy* opened at the Royal Court Theatre, London, after a successful visit to the Edinburgh Festival.

1960 30 Mar., on his 80th birthday, received greetings and tributes from all over the world. 16 June, publication of *The Drums of Father Ned* followed by British premiere. Trinity College, Dublin, offered him an honorary doctorate, which he politely refused.

1961 1 June, publication of *Behind the Green Curtains*, *Figuro in the Night*, and *The Moon Shines on Kylenamoe*. 26 July, London premiere of *The Bishop's Bonfire*.

1962 4 May, *Figuro in the Night* staged in New York. Aug.-Sept., Mermaid Theatre O'Casey Festival (*Purple Dust*, *Red Roses for Me*, *The Plough and the Stars*). 23 Oct., publication of *Feathers from the Green Crow*. 30 Oct., *Figuro in the Night* and *The Moon Shines on Klyenamoe* staged at University of Rochester, New York.

1963 3 Jan., publication of *Under a Colored Cap*. 27 Mar., Union of Soviet Writers paid tribute to O'Casey on International Theatre Day.

1964 Apr., Abbey Theatre invited to take part in World Theatre Season at the Aldwych Theatre, London, and O'Casey allowed *Juno and the Paycock* and *The Plough and the Stars* to be performed. Aug., suffered a bout of acute bronchitis. 18 Sept., died of a heart attack.

The Shadow of a Gunman

'A Tragedy in Two Acts'.
Written: 1922.
First staged: Abbey Th., Dublin, 12 Apr., 1923 (dir.
  Lennox Robinson; with Arthur Shields as Donal
  Davoren and F.J. McCormick as Seamus Shields).
Revived: Court Th., London, 27 May 1927 (dir. Arthur
  Sinclair, who also played Shields; with Harry
  Hutchinson as Davoren, Eileen Carey as Minnie
  Powell, and Sara Allgood as Mrs. Henderson);
  Martin Beck Th., New York, 30 Oct. 1932; Abbey
  Th., during 1930s; Théâtre Charles de Rochefort,
  Paris, 1947 (dir. P. Kellerson); Bijou Th., New York,
  20 Nov., 1958 (dir. Jack Garfein); Mermaid Th.,
  London, 6 Apr. 1967 (dir. Jack MacGowran);
  Komodianten, Kunsturhaus, Vienna, 27 Feb. 1976
  (dir. Conny Hans Mayer); Teatro Labortorio de
  Lisboa, Lisbon, 1976; Royal Shakespeare Company,
  The Other Place, Stratford-upon-Avon, 26 Mar.
  1980 (dir. Michael Bogdanov); Schlobparktheater,
  Frankfurt, 24 Apr. 1980 (dir. Nikolaus Haenel);
  Abbey Th., 8 May 1980 (dir. Tomas MacAnna).
Published: in *Two Plays* (London: Macmillan, 1925);
  London: Samuel French, 1932; in *Five Irish Plays*;
  in *Collected Plays I*; in *Selected Plays*; in *Three
  Plays*; and in *Complete Plays 1*. *Translated into*:
  French, German, Italian, Japanese, Persian, Polish,
  Romanian, Russian.

*A room in a tenement house, shared by Donal Davoren,
a poet, and Seamus Shields, a pedlar. The pedlar's
'Mate' appears to say he cannot go peddling that
morning, deposits a handbag to be cared for, and goes
off (as it transpires) to be killed in an ambush. Davoren
is vaguely thought to be 'on the run', and he is prepared
mildly to sustain that role to please Minnie Powell. In
Act II the tenement is raided. The handbag turns out to
contain bombs. . . Minnie takes charge of the bag: she
thinks that her room may not be searched with great*

care. However, the bombs are found, she is removed on a lorry and shot trying to escape from it.

Irish Times, Dublin, 13 Apr. 1923

[In a letter to Lennox Robinson (9 Oct. 1922), acknowledging the receipt of his returned play *The Crimson in the Tricolour*, O'Casey reveals that he is working on another, then called *On the Run*. 'It deals with the difficulties of a poet who is in continual conflict with the disturbances of a tenement house, and is built on the frame of Shelley's phrase: "Ah me, alas, pain, pain ever, forever".']

It was indeed a welcome and wholesome sign to sit in the Abbey last night and listen to an audience squirming with laughter and revelling boisterously in the satire which Mr. Sean O'Casey has put into his two-act play. Not for a very long time has such a good play come our way. It was brilliant, truthful, decisive. . . . His characters were as perfect, and his photography, for one really felt his men and women were but photographs, was nothing less than the work of genius.

Evening Herald, Dublin, 13 Apr. 1923

Mr. O'Casey's first play shows an intention similar to that of his later work. Infirmity of hand there may be, but infirmity of purpose there certainly is not. He shows us nationalism as the last refuge of poltroons and he holds up his mirror to life by the Liffey with the same anxiety to catch the reflection of the odd corner. The real hero of this play is the heroine, who could at least live up to her illusions and finally gave her life for them. She was made great by a little passion: what began as a flirtation with a dreamy poet ended as a flame which kindled an ecstatic devotion to a supposed secret soldier and mighty gunman 'on the run'. Mr. O'Casey is tolerant of Minnie Powell's romance; there was irony behind its glitter, for the poet was no gunman at all, but Minnie died to save him. Mr. O'Casey can sneer at most things, but death for a loyalty defies derision. The result is an odd, immature play. But one gets the sense of size which is so splendidly typical of this dramatist's later work.

Ivor Brown, *The Saturday Review*, 18 June 1927

It resembles his later work in its scathing sense of humour – a sense of humour that delights to present human beings in tragic circumstances, to the level of which they are ludicrously incapable of rising. . . . *The Shadow of a Gunman* reveals the Irishman once again as a creature whose imagination is too vivid to cope with ruthless fact. . . . Here is futility in action. . . . But what a brilliant, bitter human little entertainment this is! How surely it strikes the keynote of reality! The pity of it O'Casey! Oh, O'Casey, the pity of it!

Herbert Farjeon, *Graphic and National Weekly*, 11 June 1927

[In the Actors' Studio Company's revival of 1958] the tempo of the piece, up to the last minute, is exuberantly comic. . . . O'Casey belongs in the boisterous gallery of Irish satirists, comedians, ironists, and mock-heroic wits who, since the death of Shakespeare, have written nearly everything of lasting importance in what is sardonically known as the English drama. He means us to laugh at the plight of two men trapped in a lie, and he expects of his small-part players the pace and timing of vaudeville. And this is where the Actors' Studio lets him down. Instead of expedition, they give us exploration. Where O'Casey prescribes panic, they offer rational concern. Under Jack Garfein's direction, they present a number of thoughtful investigations into character, entirely ignoring the element of volatile caricature that is the glory of the play, its essence and life. Lines that in print are winged like Mercury are uttered as if they were shod in concrete.

Kenneth Tynan, *New Yorker*, 6 Dec. 1958,
reprinted in *Curtains* (London, 1961), p. 285-8

We often chase after the wrong heroes, or those who are not heroes at all. There are countless heroes in the world, but few have ribbons in their coats, which is praise to God, for he doesn't care a damn about ornaments. . . . This chasing of the hero is in the play; and also the readiness of poor conceited minds to be chased and honoured for a heroism which is often foolish; though, of course, it remains true to believe that it is good to die for one's country (people, really) should the need arise. Old Glory is often fluttered for unworthy purposes, but the flag remains a true and beautiful symbol, even when held aloft by the hands of a scoundrel. We have to pay for vain conceits; and Davoren had to pay for this.

O'Casey, letter to Ronald Gene Rollins, 30 Mar. 1959,
reprinted in *Sean O'Casey's Drama, Verisimilitude and Vision*, p. 114

In the past it has often seemed an anecdotal piece with only hints of the tragi-comic richness of the two masterpieces that followed. But it is directed by Michael Bogdanov with such atmospheric detail down to the gunshots that seem to encircle this tin-shed of a theatre [The Other Place, Stratford] that you realize it has its own dark, tragic power. ... What gives [the play] such force is the way O'Casey's principal characters combine an acute awareness of Ireland with total self deception. The pacific, Shelley-hooked Donal ruefully realizes there are plenty of Irishmen who can sleep in peace only when they've shot someone; yet he smilingly accepts the role of gunman and, in a fine directorial touch, tries on his black poet's hat in front of the mirror and then tips it over his brows to give him the look of a ruthless killer. ...

What I admire about Bogdanov's production, however, is that he doesn't steep the play in stage Oirish charm: he directs it as a tragedy. Part of the tragedy is that Donal, at 30, is still searching for his role in life; and Michael Pennington excellently plays him as a fretful drunk. Norman Rodway's Seamus gets laughs, sure, but again because of the gap between what he is and what he thinks he is; he sits on his unruly bed keening about the state of Ireland, but when he sets forth into the world he dons a Homburg and a silk scarf as if he were a masher about to take Piccadilly by storm. ... And at the end as Donal and Seamus sit in silence, lit by the flickering firelight, [Bogdanov] movingly suggests the real Irish tragedy is that self knowledge is purchased only at the expense of other people's lives.

Michael Billington, *The Guardian*, 2 Apr. 1980

[See also 'The Raid', in *Innishfallen, Fare Thee Well*, for O'Casey's autobiographical account of a Black and Tan raid on the tenement in Mountjoy Square in which he shared a room with Michael O'Maolain during 1920, and O'Maolain's own account, 'The Raid and What Went With It', trans. Maureen Murphy, in *Essays on Sean O'Casey's Autobiographies*, ed. Robert G. Lowery.]

Cathleen Listens In

'A Phantasy in One Act'.
Written: 1922.
First performed: Abbey Th., 1 Oct. 1923 (dir. Lennox Robinson); revived in revised version, 3 Mar. 1925.

Published: in *Tulane Drama Review*, June 1961. Revised version in *Feathers from the Green Crow*; and in *Complete Plays 5*. *Translated into*: German.

Cathleen, daughter of Miceawl Houlihan, symbolizes Ireland. She is courted by several suitors representing the various political groupings interested in the country's future – a Free Stater, a Republican, a Business Man. Cathleen remains indifferent to their advances, preferring to spend her time 'listenin' in' to the wireless, until they wear her down and she faints. The doctor prescribes 'perfect peace and quietness for the rest of her National life' if the attack is not to prove fatal.

[In his autobiography O'Casey describes the piece as 'a jovial, sardonic sketch on the various parties in conflict over Irish politics – Sinn Fein, Free State, and Labour'. Cathleen of the title refers to Cathleen ni Houlihan, the symbolic name for Ireland.]

The new play . . . calls itself a Phantasy, and is not, we imagine taking itself very seriously as a play; but it invites some serious consideration as an allegory, or perhaps we might say a rough-and-tumble morality play. . . . The mordant idea of the play is found in the spectral Gaelic League, under the figure of a feeble old man in kilts – who receives solemn homage from the actors, whenever he appears, but is voted a nuisance and a lunatic when his back is turned. The climax of comedy is reached when at the height of the shouting of the claimants for Cathleen's suffrages the Boundary Question stalks by outside playing on a big drum the appropriate air.

Irish Statesman, 6 Oct. 1923

O'Casey's new play . . . has been a success – though the first night it seemed . . . above the heads of its audience. As soon as the latter had realized its type, however, as the week went on, they expressed their approval warmly. . . . It is a somewhat unorthodox kind of trifle . . . but it has breadth and depth and vitality enough for its scope.

The Evening Telegraph, Dublin, 6 Oct. 1923

Juno and the Paycock

'A Tragedy in Three Acts'.
Written: 1923.
First performed: Abbey Th., Dublin, 3 Mar. 1924 (dir. Michael
J. Dolan; with Barry Fitzgerald as Boyle, Sara Allgood as
Juno, and F.J. McCormick as Joxer).
Revived: Royalty Th., London, 16 Nov. 1925 (dir. J.B. Fagan;
with Arthur Sinclair as Boyle, Sara Allgood as Juno, and
Sydney Morgan as Joxer); Mayfair Th., New York, 15 Mar.
1926 (dir. Augustin Duncan); annually at Abbey Th. until
1939 (except 1936); Mansfield Th., New York, 16 Dec. 1940
(dir. Arthur Shields); Théâtre de l'Oeuvre, Paris, 1950 (dir.
P. Kellerson); National Th., Reykyavik, 1952; World Theatre
Season (Abbey Th. Company), Aldwych Th., London, 1964;
National Th. at Old Vic, London, 26 Apr. 1966 (dir. Laurence
Olivier); Mermaid Th., London, 2 Jul. 1973 (dir. and des.
Sean Kenny; with Siobhan McKenna as Juno); Mark Taper
Forum, Los Angeles, 7 Nov. 1974 (dir. George Seaton; with
Walter Matthau as Boyle and Jack Lemmon as Joxer);
Schiller-Theater, Berlin, 21 Dec. 1974 (dir. Hans Lietzau);
Burgtheater, Vienna, 16 June 1977 (dir. Otto Scheuk); RSC,
Aldwych Th., London, 1 Oct. 1980 (dir. Trevor Nunn; des.
John Gunter; with Judi Dench as Juno and Norman Rodway
as Boyle); Citizens' Th., Glasgow, 21 Oct. 1983 (dir.
Giles Havergal).
Published: in *Two Plays* (London: Macmillan, 1925); London:
Macmillan, 1928; in *Five Irish Plays*; London: Macmillan,
1948 (Scholar's Library); in *Collected Plays I*; in *Selected
Plays*; in *Three Plays*; in *The Sean O'Casey Reader*; in *Six
Plays*; and in *Complete Plays 1*.
Translated into: Arabic, Chinese, Danish, Dutch, French,
German, Hungarian, Italian, Portuguese, Romanian, Russian,
Spanish, Swedish, Turkish.

---

*'On a little by-road off Finglas way it was, he was found.' ...
The words were spoken by way of gossip by Mary Boyle, the only
daughter of a family resident in a Dublin tenement. She had just
been reading the paper ... and at the time she spoke she was
trying to decide whether a blue or a green riband would look best
in her hair. For Mary was on strike, and therefore out of work,*

and therefore also had more time for dressing up and gadding about and supping on the sensations in the daily papers. Mary's father was Jack Boyle, called 'Captain' by his intimates of the public house snuggery, because once on a time he sailed a tramp from the Liffey to Liverpool. Since when he was on the rocks, and never wanted to get off. Mary's mother was called Juno because – well, because it was as good as July. Mary's brother was Johnny, a boy who 'done his bit' in the Tan days and in the 1922 days, and who was now seeking to get away from his conscience with an arm gone and a bomb bullet in his hip, lying about the house like a ghost in chains hearing and fearing the presence of ghosts unchained. To this home of mischances and misfits it was Juno who brought the bacon – the feeding and the drinking. But fortune turned. A relative, up Santry way, conveniently died, leaving the head of the Boyle family a small fortune. And to celebrate the occasion a 'hooley' is given. Friends are invited, including 'Joxer' Daly the champion 'toucher' of the tenement, and also Charlie Bentham, a school teacher, who had brought first news of the timely passing of the wealthy kinsman, and who was wooing Mary with all the enthusiasm of the follower of an heiress. It was to and through this tenement, while corks popped from porter bottles and the air rang with raucous song and gramophone ribaldry, that tragedy stalked. Another resident of the tenement was 'waking' the corpse of her son. And amid the cries and prayers that rose from her harrowed heart we gathered that her dead son had been leader of an ambush when a neighbour's son in the National Army had been killed. Fate followed fast. The fortune was a fake. The Boyle family became bankrupt and bailiff ridden. Mary, betrayed by her banished lover, was sheltered by the mother, cursed by the father, and reviled by the brother. And this same brother, held suspect by his brother 'die-hards' . . . was brought out at the muzzle of the rifle and heard no more. . . . Making allowances for the author's thirst for dialogue with a dig in it, this play stands as one of the greatest things done by the Abbey players.

'Jacques', *Irish Independent*, 4 Mar. 1924

March 8 1924. In the evening to the Abbey with W.B. Yeats, *Juno and the Paycock* – a long queue at the door, the theatre crowded,

21

many turned away, so it will run on next week. A wonderful and terrible play of futility, of irony, humour, tragedy. When I went round to the green-room I saw Casey and had a little talk with him. He is very happy. . . . And he said, 'I owe a great deal to you and Mr. Yeats and Mr. Robinson, but to you above all. And it was you who said to me upstairs in the office – I could show you the very spot where you stood – "Mr. Casey, your gift is characterization". And so I threw over my theories and worked at characters and this is the result.'
Lady Gregory's Journals 1916-1930, p. 74-5

The spectacle of the Abbey crammed to the doors on the first week in Lent is eloquent of the fascinations of his curiously-composite dramaturgy. He has been the means of showing us . . . that what the great public hungers after is not poetic or historical drama, not even peasant drama, but the drama of palpitating city life. Democracy has at last become articulate on both sides of the curtain. . . .

Mr. O'Casey is at once iconoclastic and neo-Elizabethan. One cannot place his plays in any recognized category. Nothing in Polonious's breathless, jaw-breaking list applies; and he flouts all the precepts of Aristotle. He lures us into the theatre under the pretext of affording us hearty laughter, which, sooth to say, he most profusely provokes, and he sends us away with tears in our eyes and with the impression of direst tragedy lying heavy on our hearts. None but a neo-Elizabethan could accomplish this, since the secret of juxtaposing and harmonizing the comic with the tragic, and thereby throwing the elements of terror and pathos into greater relief, has been lost to the English-speaking stage for over a couple of centuries. Moreover, one-half of the fascination of Mr. O'Casey's work lies in its red-hot throbbing contemporaneity, and that too was a prime trait of Elizabethan drama. There are moments in his plays . . so vivid in the light of recent experience that they transcend all mere theatricality and thrill one to the marrow like matters of personal suffering.
W.J. Lawrence, *The Irish Statesman*, 15 Mar. 1924

Juno and the Paycock is as much a tragedy as Macbeth, but it is a tragedy taking place in the porter's family.
James Agate, *Sunday Times*, 16 Nov. 1925
(review reprinted in full in *Sean O'Casey: Modern Judgements*, ed. Ronald Ayling, p. 76-8)

Captain Boyle can hardly be overdrawn. [Barry] Fitzgerald's notion of this raffish tenement charlatan of Dublin is fantastically comic. Dressed in wrinkled rags that cling uncertainly to his portly figure, a huge belt carelessly buckled around his waist, a squalid cap at an angle on his head, Captain Boyle is stern and pompous on the surface and all bluff underneath. . . . Mr. Fitzgerald's tightly-drawn face is an essential part of his portrait – querulous and alarmed by turns; and his voice plays tunes on the character. Sometimes it rises to the singsong of public speaking. Captain Boyle is a part that Mr. Fitzgerald enjoys. He has played it so long that he has filled out all the lines of O'Casey's racy drawing. It is one of the theatre's modern masterpieces.

Although the part of Juno is less spectacular, Miss Allgood's hot-tempered playing reaches down all through Mr. O'Casey's drama and stirs up some of the groundswell of feeling that should be there. In Miss Allgood's acting Juno is a strong character – swift of foot and mind, with the remnants of middle-class respectability coming instinctively to life on social occasions.

A tatterdemalion in her dress and a shrew in speech, she is a mother in the protection she instinctively gives to her children, and she never forgets to straighten her hair and smooth down her apron when she answers a knock on the door. The tragic scenes at the close of the play Miss Allgood acts with an anguish that gets closer to the heart of O'Casey's drama than anything else in the performance.

Brooks Atkinson, *New York Times*, 17 Jan. 1940

Realistic would not be quite the right word to describe this piece, nor naturalistic; I think 'life-like' would be nearer the mark. Though there is fantasy in the characters, I feel O'Casey wished the play itself to be kept out of that realm. Poetic, of course, it is, but in its time it was felt to be very actual, as naturalistic as you could very well go in the early 'twenties, with 'good' lines and a generous portion of rhetoric. . . . It is, in fact, closer to Osborne than to Chekhov. There is no playing about with it, it is all there and it as clear as daylight what he wants done with it. What is it makes the characters so immediately recognizable and familiar and at the same time freshly minted, I wonder? The play deals in eternals and there isn't a character who hasn't made a turning-point mistake in his life. . . .

Its switchback ride between hilarity and extreme pathos puts me in mind of a definition by Miss Rose Brennan, the Irish singer, of an Irish 'hooley'. 'In the middle of all the fun somebody will get up and sing a nostalgic song and before you can say Ballaghaderreen we're all crying in our beer. The whole essence of a hooley is this sudden switch from hilarity to sadness and the equally sudden explosion back to noise, song and laughter.' . . . I think just possibly O'Casey might have described *Juno* as a 'hooley'.

Laurence Olivier, programme note to his production
for the National Theatre, 1966

They may burn my effigy in Dublin for saying so, but the play gains enormously from [Olivier's] placing of it in a British tradition and atmosphere. To fill the large Old Vic stage, he's stolen for it the setting of *The Plough and the Stars*: instead of a tenement room, the Boyle family now inhabit a huge, tatterdemalion Georgian salon from whose dim grandeurs loom the music-hall faces of a Sickert canvas. The strong, simple line Olivier takes is one of thriller-comedy. The Boyle family's fortune and humours ebb and flow across a stage dominated at the rear by the dark inner space where armless Johnnie shudders with guilt and terror before the figure of the Virgin, waiting for the Furies in trench-coats to come and claim him. It's a reading which reflects the peculiar strengths of his cast. Colin Blakely is superb as Boyle, a hard little cork of vanity bobbing on a sea of troubles, his faded ginger bullet-head unbowed, save in delicate flickers of uncertainty when his ignorance is exposed. Frank Finlay at present is slightly too finicky as Joxer, but a splendidly parasitical presence: a sharp-nosed, weak-eyed grey shadow at Blakely's heel.

They're matched on the tragic side by the strength of Ronald Pickup's Johnnie. In one of Olivier's best simplifications, he sleepwalks chalk-faced through a flurry of comic panic by Finlay and Blakely, clearing the stage for his killers. . . .

Olivier's straightforward, British emphasis misses an Irish undercurrent which runs powerfully counter to O'Casey's surface anti-clericalism – the Catholic pathos for all womanhood. The crucial entrance of the widow Tancred, on her way with her mourners to her son's funeral, is muted, played almost off-stage. The charge of emotion it should accumulate for Juno's final speech is lost. We must wait for another revival, with another Sara Allgood, to judge whether O'Casey achieved his real ambition for the play: to make a slum Pieta.

Ronald Bryden, The Observer, 1 May 1966

Outrageous claims have been made for *Juno and the Paycock* – not least by Yeats who told Lady Gregory that the play reminded him of a Dostoievsky novel. 'You know, Willie', she said, 'you never read a novel by Dostoievsky'. Her caution is printed early in the National Theatre programme and one can see why. No nonsense for Olivier about the sacred travail of womanhood, Ireland's cavalry, her answer to the Greeks, the tragic masterpiece of the century, etc.; and none of the stifling piety which made the Abbey Theatre's *Juno*, in London two years ago, so woefully boring. His production firmly charts the rise and fall of a great comic hero, according to the strictest classic pattern. . . . News of his inheritance comes as no surprise – beyond his wildest dreams perhaps, but to such a practised dreamer it is no trouble to adjust them. The full glory of his transformation emerges in Act Two when, encased in tweeds and watch-chain, he sets himself to perform the novel rites of capitalist and genial paterfamilias. Chaffing Joxer from a great height, gently rebuking Juno, chatting man-to-man with puzzled Mr. Bentham about consols and yogi in the streets of San Francisco – everything he does is weird and grand, in keeping with the solemnity of his elevation to the bourgeoisie. Tetchiness has vanished in a radiant benevolence. He rocks on his heels, crooks his little finger, subdues his natural bellow to strangled hiccups of pleasure after the recital of his party piece. He is genteel to a point beyond absurdity – a man reverently living a myth.

His exposure in Act Three – heralded by a long pause, a characteristic Olivier mood change, when the empty stage is filled by the heavy sounds of Mr. Blakely breathing and the occasional gurgle of stout – comes as the inexorable turning of the comic mills.

Hilary Spurling, *The Spectator*, 6 May 1966

[Judi Dench's Juno in the RSC centenary revival of 1980 was] a wonderful blend of exhaustion and despair. Tiny gestures, like a cynical lift of the eyes when the Captain starts his seafaring nonsense, speak volumes; yet there is also in the very way she plumps the cushion, stokes the fire, or makes the breakfast the suggestion of a woman who finds what solace she can in routine. . . . [Norman Rodway] the work-shy paycock . . . was from the start both chicken and vain. One notes the devious, backhand way he slips a sausage into the pan having proclaimed he wants no breakfast, the mad light that comes into his eyes when he talks of his non-existent sea-faring, even the way he swells visibly in his chair when he thinks he is the beneficiary of a will. It is a lovely performance, splendidly partnered by John Rogan's sly, ingratiating Joxer bubbling with ill-suppressed glee at his partner's downfall: a Silence to Rodway's Justice Shallow.

Michael Billington, *The Guardian*, 8 Oct. 1980

Gerard Murphy conveys the agony of the trapped young son, waiting for the fatal knock at the door and surrounded by his tense but equally confused family. Mr. Murphy, like everyone else in the play, has the rare ability of being able to listen as well as to speak; without hamming it up, he gives a memorable performance, intent upon each idiocy of irrelevance explored by his family as he rests uncomfortably on the bed at the side of the room. Dearbhla Molloy gives the essence of an eager confused girl as Mary: her scenes with her first lover, so intelligently played by Frank Grimes, have a perfectly phrased dignity. Marie Kean combines dignity with absolute desolation as the neighbouring mother whose son is killed, and whose speech of pained acceptance presages Juno's stoic utterance at the end of the play.

Bryan Robertson, *The Spectator*, 18 Oct. 1980

. . . But no sooner has she (Juno) gone to identify her son's corpse, and then to nurse her daughter through a 'shameful' pregnancy, than on totter the two idlers and topers, mouthing what to them are no more than platitudes about the world's 'chassis'. Only O'Casey, for whom pain and foible, comedy and tragedy were inseparable, could have composed a scene of such bitter hilarity and then left it to lurch and cackle round our skulls.

Benedict Nightingale, *New Statesman*, 17 Oct. 1980

It is a tragedy of vanity, and of subservience to vanity. There is a touch of Boyle in all of us. We strut along thinking that our shadows shine. There's a touch of Joxer in a lot of us: saying yes where we ought to say no. And I hope there is some Mrs. Boyle in all of us. To be brave even at the eleventh hour.

O'Casey writing in 1955, quoted in the programme for the RSC production

Nannie's Night Out

'A Comedy in One Act.'
Written: 1924.
First performed: Abbey Th., Dublin, 29 Sept. 1924 (dir. Michael J. Dolan).
Revived: Little Th., Lafayette, Indiana, 13 Mar. 1961 (dir. Robert Hogan); Kleine Komodie im Kulturpalast, Dresden, 1973 (dir. Helfried Schobel). No professional production recorded in England.

Published: in *Feathers from the Green Crow*; and in *Complete Plays 5. Translated into*: French, German.

Irish Nannie, a destitute meths drinker and mother of a hunchbacked son, roams the streets of Dublin 'very near to hysterical tears', while Polly Pender, the respectable owner of the local dairy, is courted by three buffoon suitors. An armed burglar breaks into the dairy and holds Polly and her men to ransom, but Nannie, on a drunken spree, 'rushes in like a whirlwind' and courageously frightens him off. O'Casey offers two endings: Nannie dying of a heart attack, or the police dragging her off to gaol.

The Plough and the Stars

'A Tragedy in Four Acts'.
Written: 1924-25.
First performed: Abbey Th., Dublin, 8 Feb., 1926 (dir. Lennox Robinson; with Barry Fitzgerald as Fluther Good, Shelah Richards as Nora Clitheroe, and F.J. McCormick as Jack Clitheroe).
Revived: Fortune Th., London, 12 May 1926 (dir. J.B. Fagan; with Arthur Sinclair as Fluther, Sara Allgood as Bessie Burgess, and Eileen Carey as Nora); Hudson Th., New York, 27 Nov. 1927 (with Arthur Sinclair and Sara Allgood); annually at the Abbey Th. until 1940, and in the 1950s (dir. Ria Mooney, the original Rosie Redmond); Mermaid Th., London, 25 Sept. 1962 (dir. Joss Ackland); Comédie de Saint-Etienne, Théâtre Montparnasse, Paris, May 1962 (dir. Jean Dasté); World Theatre Season (Abbey Theatre Company) Aldwych Th., London, 1964; Hans-Otto Theater, Potsdam, 1972 (dir. Rolf Winkelgrund); Toronto Arts Productions Theatre Company, 26 Nov. 1975 (dir. Martin Kinch); Abbey Th., Dublin, 14 May 1976 (dir. Thomas MacAnna; with Cyril Cusack as Fluther and Siobhan McKenna as Bessie); National Th., London, 20 Sept. 1977 (dir. Bill Bryden; with Cyril Cusack as Fluther, Anna Manahan as Bessie, and J.G. Devlin as Uncle Peter); Lyric Th., Belfast, 7 Nov. 1977 (dir. Conor O'Malley); Royal Exchange Th., Manchester, 8 Feb. 1984 (dir. Gregory Hersov).

Film version: released Jan. 1937, (dir. John Ford; with Barbara Stanwyck as Nora, Barry Fitzgerald as Fluther, and Eileen Crowe as Bessie).

Published: London: Macmillan, 1926; in *Five Irish Plays*; London: Macmillan, 1948 (Scholar's Library); in *Collected Plays I*; in *Selected Plays*; in *Three Plays*; in *The Sean O'Casey Reader*; in *Six Plays*; in *Literature from the Irish Literary Revival* (Washington: University Press of America, 1982); and in *Complete Plays 1*. *Translated into*: Arabic, French, German, Italian, Japanese, Romanian, Russian, Spanish.

The title refers to the flag of the Irish Citizen Army which, with the Irish Volunteers, spearheaded the Easter Rising in 1916. The impact of the insurrection on the lives of the Dublin people is seen through the experience of a group of tenement dwellers, in particular those for whom the event has tragic consequences, newly-weds Jack and Nora Clitheroe and their indomitable neighbour, Bessie Burgess. Despite Nora's pleading, Jack, motivated by vanity and false idealism, accepts promotion to Commandant in the ICA and fights in the rebellion. As a result Nora loses her husband, her unborn child, and finally her reason. Bessie – whose fierce protestantism and normally vicious manner are often a source of conflict between her and her neighbours – shows great courage and generosity of spirit in her concern and care for Nora, until she is shot dead trying to protect her from a cross-fire of bullets, and becomes another unnecessary human sacrifice claimed by the Rising. As the British troops occupy the burning city, the other residents – life-embracing Fluther Good, pseudo-Socialist Young Covey, irascible old Peter Flynn, and gossipy Mrs. Gogan – are spared, save for Mrs. Gogan's daughter Mollser who dies of consumption, victim of the other ever-present evil, poverty.

[In spite of a good reception for the first three performances, at the fourth (11 Feb.) an organized demonstration led by Mrs. Sheehy Skeffington (whose husband was shot during the Easter Rising) degenerated into a riot during which 'about twenty ardent young women and a few young men did their best to pull the curtains down, swinging from them and kicking over the footlights' (Stephen Gwynn,

The Observer, 14 Feb. 1926). As the noise from the audience increased the actors were reduced to performing in virtual dumb-show and during Act III the performance was called to a halt. The curtain went up on 'a stiff, pompous and furious Yeats' who remonstrated with the audience as he had done fifteen years earlier on the occasion of the riots which greeted J.M. Synge's *The Playboy of the Western World*.] I thought you had got tired of this, which you commenced fifteen years ago. But you have disgraced yourselves again. Is this going to be a recurring celebration of Irish genius? Synge first and then O'Casey. The news of the happening of the last few minutes here will flash from country to country. Dublin has again rocked the cradle of genius. From such a scene as this went forth the fame of Synge. Equally the fame of O'Casey is born here tonight. This is his apotheosis.

W.B. Yeats, reprinted in Robert G. Lowery,
A Whirlwind in Dublin (1984), p. 31

[Eventually the police were called, the demonstrators left the theatre and the performance continued. For a detailed account of what took place see Hugh Hunt, *The Abbey: Ireland's National Theatre, 1904-1979* (Dublin: Gill and Macmillan, 1979) and Robert G. Lowery, *A Whirlwind in Dublin* (Greenwood Press, 1984).]

The demonstration was not directed against the individual actor, nor was it directed to the moral aspect of the play. It was on national grounds solely, voicing a passionate indignation against the outrage of a drama staged in a supposedly national theatre, which held up to derision and obloquy the men and women of Easter week.

The protest was made, not by Republicans alone, and had the sympathy of large numbers in the house. There is a point beyond which toleration becomes merely servility, and realism not art, but morbid perversity. The play, as a play, may be left to the judgement of posterity, which will rank it as artistically far below some of Mr. O'Casey's work. It is the realism that would paint not only the wart on Cromwell's nose, but that would add carbuncles and running sores in a reaction against idealization. In no country save in Ireland could a state-subsidized theatre presume on popular patience to the extent of making a mockery and a byword of a revolutionary movement on which the present structure claims to stand.

Mrs. Sheehy-Skeffington, letter to
Irish Independent, 15 Feb. 1926

[The full text of this and a subsequent letter from Mrs. Skeffington, and of O'Casey's replies, are reprinted in *The Letters of Sean O'Casey, Volume I, 1910-1941*, p. 167-80.]

Feb. 14, Sunday. On Friday I left for Dublin to see *The Plough and the Stars.* . . . I thought the play very fine indeed. And the next day at the matinee, when, though the house was full and overflowing, there was no danger of riot and I could listen without distraction, it seemed to a me a very wonderful play – 'the forgiveness of sins', as real literature is supposed to be. These quarrelling, drinking women have tenderness and courage, showing all through, as have the men. At intervals in the public-house scene one hears from the meeting being held outside fragments of a speech of Pearse (spoken in Stephenson's fine voice with extraordinary effect). One feels those who heard it were forced to obey its call, not to be afraid to fight even in the face of defeat. One honours and understands their emotions. . . . And then comes what all nations have seen, the suffering that falls through war, and especially civil war, on the women, the poor, the wretched homes and families of the slums. An overpowering play. I felt at the end of it as if I should never care to look at another; all others would seem shadowy to the mind after this.
Lady Gregory's Journals, 1916-1930, p. 95-9

I have more than once described Mr. O'Casey as an Irish Chekhov, and I abide by that description, but I might more aptly describe him as a sentimental Hogarth, a Hogarth without any savagery in him. Mr. O'Casey, who must have found himself in congenial company the other night when he sat by the side of Mr. Augustus John, paints his pictures with the same veracity that Hogarth painted his, but he has not Hogarth's insane detachment from his subjects. If anything is manifest in [the plays] it is the immense pity and love which Mr. O'Casey feels for the people in the tenements. They are offered to us without any middle-class palliation or contempt – a fact which no doubt accounts for the hysterical wrath of the refined ladies who kicked up a hullabaloo in the Abbey – and are neither condemned nor exalted. There they are, as they are and for what they are, creatures full of vanity and windy emotions, child-like, superstitious, senti-mental, kindly, greedy, full of ferocity and fear, capable of courage, play-acting, and a sour sort of romance; and with it all, pitiable. They have their strutting vanity, and their mouths are full of wrecked words, lost in Ireland when the Elizabethan tradition foundered in the appalling mess of industrialism in England; but they have, too, a comic dignity and glory which raises them above their sordid circumstances and relates them to the age of romance and the swaggering grace of men who still possess rights in their own minds. That is why these people, as they are offered to us by Mr. O'Casey, steal into our affections, even while we are informing each other that they are hopeless and can never be regenerate.

St. John Ervine, *The Observer*, 16 May 1927

The prime quality of Mr. O'Casey's work is that, though hardly a moment passes on the stage which does not drive home some stroke of satire or humour and make us laugh, the effect of each scene as a whole is disturbing and grave. As in the case of almost every play about Irish character, his effects are chiefly based upon the contrast between the shining qualities which the characters attribute to themselves and their actual behaviour. . . .

The second act is the finest act Mr. O'Casey has written. In the scene in the pub he has expressed his theme perfectly. Through the large window to the left of the bar come intermittent wafts of idealistic rebel oratory . . . while inside Fluther, the Covey, Mrs. Gogan, Bessie, Peter, and the little prostitute, Rosie, squabble and rant and drink. It is a scene of excellent and mordant comedy.

Desmond MacCarthy, *New Statesman*, 29 May 1926

Mr. O'Casey has done what Balzac and Dickens did – he has created an entirely new gallery of living men and women. . . . You may be appalled, but you do not blame; these people are alive, and you refrain from judging them. . . . [The play] moves to its tragic close through scenes of high humour and rich, racy fooling, about which there is something of Elizabethan gusto. Young Covey roars his gospel of economic regeneration with the emphasis of Pistol; there is a Falstaffian ring about Fluther, mercurial excitability taking the place of the lethargic sweep; old Flynn is Shallow all over again; and Rose is pure Doll. . . .

It may be that the first two acts are something meandering, and that at the end of them we feel that though we have been tremendously amused the piece has not got sufficiently under way. This is largely owing to the fact that Mr. O'Casey's people talk too much but not dramatically enough. . . . Despite the confusion there is a fine dramatic meal in this play. There is a magnificent passage in the public-house, in which the officers of the Citizen Army pledge themselves to imprisonment, wounds, and death. They go out, and then Rosie and Fluther enact a scene of dalliance which might be a pendant to the amours of the fat knight [Falstaff] and his mistress.

James Agate, *Sunday Times*, 16 May 1926

Tragedy, it says in the programme [to the first French production of 1962]. Indeed it is one, but not in the sense which this word generally has in France. In what he says about his production, about his understanding of the play, Jean Dasté forcefully emphasises a complexity which runs somewhat counter to our normal habits as theatregoers. For we have many opportunities to laugh during this tragedy, rather as one might laugh at a farce; many opportunities to shed tears, rather like one may at a melodrama. . . .

There are no general ideas about revolt for its own sake nor about abstract freedom. O'Casey only ever talks about what he knows, understands, and feels the best; which, in this case, means the resonances that a 'historic' event, this uprising for example, can have on a small group of individuals, all very different from one another, whom he knows, who are people who live in his area, who have no vocation for 'making history' and yet who participate in history, each according to his temperament, his character – according to a personality which organized political parties want to have nothing to do with, which they detest. It is precisely those characters which fascinate O'Casey and which he is capable of making magnificently vivid and true to life. . . . It is a whole world, secret, absurd, noble, which the combined art of O'Casey and Jean Dasté open for us. It sounds like a serialized story which one cannot 'put down'.

Jacques Lemarchand, *Le Figaro Litteraire*,
Paris, 12 May 1962, trans. Colin Boswell

This is a tragedy which makes you laugh a lot, a comedy which ends with four dead bodies . . . a tragedy which has no kings and queens, but instead a builder, a fitter, a carpenter, a cleaning lady, and a few other representatives of the Dublin working class. A comedy which is not about adultery or seduction, but about the Irish people's struggle for independence.

I am talking of tragedy and of comedy in order to give, so to speak, some intellectual landmarks, for O'Casey's plays cannot be so easily pigeon-holed. The name of Brecht often crops up, but if one really must compare to anyone then it would be to Chekhov, especially in his ability to create an atmosphere and to make his characters come to life with an amazing verisimilitude.

Guy Leclerc, *L'Humanité*,
Paris, 1 May 1962, trans. Colin Boswell

Cyril Cusack ... fluttered more than a feather of the traditional Fluther Good. He built the role so gently, offering the richly comic lines as the ordinary colloquialisms of a quiet, decent Dubliner, that its impact had a delayed-action mechanism built into it. It came finally and surely, not like a thunderclap, but as a catch in the throat and an enormous wave of affection from the audience. This was great acting.

Other variations were of emphasis rather than a fundamental rethinking, such as Siobhan McKenna's portrayal of Bessie Burgess with a Northern accent. It was legitimate enough – she is, at one point, called an Orange bitch – and tended to underline her alienation from the 1916 rebels and their sympathizers.

Gerry Colgan, *Hibernia*, Dublin, 4 June 1976

The play still stands for me as the greatest of the Irish theatre in my time, and as the finest of that inspired recorder's reports on the Dublin people he lived with and the Dublin that he lived in through some of its most dramatic years. . . . Miss McKenna is the first Bessie I've seen who essayed a Northern accent in the part. Nothing in O'Casey's stage directions suggest this, and while it is allowable for Dolphie Grigson [the Orangeman in *Shadow of a Gunman*] it seems to me a dubious twist for a woman who is the quintessence of Moore Street.

Seamus Kelly, *Irish Times*, 15 May 1976

In its neighbourly way, it spreads a tapestry of local colour, meaning to make its anti-war point by sacrificing the humanity of everyday life to the arbitrary bloodshed of war. This point is mainly made through the marriage of Jack and Nora Clitheroe. In the play's best scene, early on, they are lovingly portrayed as a close and loving pair. They are also doomed to tragedy, so obviously that the entire play is marred by the predictability of this central (and just about only) event.

Because this couple exists basically to be destroyed, there was little motivation for the author to give them personal characteristics and as a result the leading role falls to Fluther Good, who hasn't much to do with the story. He is, however, the repository of all the Irish qualities that O'Casey loved best. In effect, Fluther is the Ireland that the bloodshed is destroying. The author fills him with great love and I've never seen him played badly. It's a grand role and Cyril Cusack does a wonderful job.

Martin Gottfried, *New York Post*, 18 Nov. 1976

The case for O'Casey is readily put. Few playwrights, other than Shakespeare, have had such an easy mastery of the special texture of tragi-comedy. O'Casey can make you laugh with a sob in your throat. Also, his characters – in his best plays at least – seem to have walked into the theatre appropriately bewildered and bedazzled from some Dublin street.

The case against him is equally clear. While he has a sure feel for dramatic tone his sense of dramatic structure is far less secure. And his willingness to wring the heartstrings of his audience at times carries him over the brink into sentimentality. There can be too many death scenes, too many cleverly contrived contrasts that are like theatrical chiaroscuro, effective in places but cumulatively overpowering.

The characters are fantasticated yet totally true in their theatrical sense. . . . And the situations are bold and effective, even when, until the slap-bang finale, slightly inconclusive.

This anniversary, bicentenniel production, directed by Tomas MacAnna, has been lovingly and beautifully staged. There is a sense of tradition here that enables the play to work with the conscious stylistic confidence of an opera. The actors move around one another with a friendly virtuosity, and voices blend in with one another like the cries of seagulls on Galway Bay.

Clive Barnes, *New York Times*, 18 Nov. 1976

The Silver Tassie

'A Tragi-Comedy in Four Acts'.
Written: 1926-28.
First performed: Apollo Th., London, 11 Oct. 1929
(dir. Raymond Massey; des. Gladys Calthorp and Augustus John (Act II); with Charles Laughton as Harry Heegan, Barry Fitzgerald as Sylvester Heegan, and Sidney Morgan as Simon Norton).
Revived: Irish Th., New York, 24 Oct. 1929 (dir. Miceal Breathnach; des. Charles Friedman); Abbey Th., Dublin, 12 Aug. 1935 (dir. Arthur Shields; with F.J. McCormick as Harry, Eileen Crowe as Susie Monican, and Cyril Cusack as one of the soldiers); Interplayers Theatre, Carnegie Hall, 21 July 1949 (dir. Al Saxe; with Jack Palance as Harry); Schauspielhaus, Zurich, 8 Nov. 1952 (dir. Berthold Viertel); Schillertheater, Berlin, 20 June 1953 (dir. Fritz Kortner; des. Caspar Neher); Volkstheater, Vienna, 19 Jan. 1954 (dir. Leon Epp); Playhouse, Nottingham, Apr. 1967 (dir. John Neville;

des. Patrick Robertson); La Guilde, Théâtre de L'Est
Parisien, Apr. 1967 (dir. Guy Retoré); Royal Shakespeare
Company, Aldwych Th., London, 10 Sept. 1969 (dir. David
Jones; des. John Bury; with Helen Mirren as Susie and Ben
Kingsley as the Croucher); Abbey Th., Dublin, 27 Sept. 1972
(dir. Hugh Hunt); Th. Royal, Stratford East, London,
9 Feb. 1977 (dir. Clare Venables).

Published: London; Macmillan, 1928; in *Collected Plays II*; in
Selected Plays; in *Three More Plays*; in *The Sean O'Casey
Reader*; and in *Complete Plays 2*. (The 'stage version', first
printed in *Collected Plays* was the result of considerable
revision of the text by O'Casey after the play had been
produced in London.) *Translated into*: French, German,
Italian, Slovak.

*Harry Heegan, football hero and winner of the cup (the silver
tassie) for the Avondale Club, returns to Dublin from the First
World War maimed and bitter. He loses his girl Jessie to his best
friend Barney Bagnal, who has been awarded the VC for saving
Harry's life. Harry's family and friends (including Susie
Monican, once in love with him) are unable to understand or
alleviate his suffering; only Teddy Foran, Harry's neighbour
and fellow casualty who has experienced the horror of war and
its terrible consequence, is able to give him some comfort. At the
football club dance Harry, now confined permanently to a
wheelchair, rages impotently against his condition and destroys
the tassie, symbol of his former triumphs. He leaves with his
parents and Teddy, while those who have witnessed his anguish,
with unease but apparent incomprehension, return to the dance.
The spirit of war is vividly conveyed by the awesome nightmare
vision of Act II.*

I've just finished writing . . . *The Silver Tassie*. . . . I'll send a copy to
The Abbey, and will send a copy to no-one else till I get word that the
play has been received, so that I may be able to say that The Abbey
Theatre was the first to get my new effort. I hope it may be suitable,
and that you will like it. Personally, I think the play is the best work
that I have done. I have certainly put my best into it, and have written
the work solely because of love and a deep feeling that what I have
written should have been written. . . . Most of the Second Act is to be

sung. A good deal to Gregorian chant, and some to the airs of songs and a hymn. . . . There's no mention of politics throughout the play.

O'Casey, letter to Lady Gregory, 28 Feb. 1928

My dear Casey . . . You have no subject. You were interested in the Irish civil war, and at every moment of those plays wrote out or your own amusement with life of your sense of its tragedy; you were excited, and we all caught your excitement; you were exasperated almost beyond endurance by what you had seen or heard as a man is by what happens under his window, and you moved us as Swift moved his contemporaries. But you are not interested in the Great War; you never stood on its battlefields or walked its hospitals, and so you write out of your opinions. You illustrate those opinions by a series of almost unrelated scenes as you might in a leading article; there is no dominating character, no dominating action, neither psychological unity nor unity of action, and your great power of the past has been the creation of some unique character who dominated all about him and was himself a main impulse in some action that filled the play from beginning to end. The mere greatness of the world war has thwarted you; it has refused to become mere background, and obtrudes itself upon the stage as so much dead wood that will not burn dramatic fire. Dramatic action is a fire that must burn everything but itself; there should be no room in a play for anything that does not belong to it; the whole history of the world must be reduced to wallpaper in front of which the characters must pose and speak.

W.B. Yeats, letter to O'Casey, 20 April 1928

[On 30 April O'Casey received the Abbey directorate's decision to reject the play in a letter from Lady Gregory. She included other correspondence which had passed between her, Yeats, and Lennox Robinson in the hope that it would make clear to O'Casey why the play had been rejected and suggest to him how he might cope with the consequences.]

The rejection of the play was not unexpected – I have said many times to some friends – had a bet about it in fact – to my wife . . . and even to Barry Fitzgerald when he was here, that I thought that the play wouldn't be fondled by the Abbey. Lady Gregory in her kind way again enclosed portion of a letter from W.B. Yeats which unfolds the suggestion that the directorate would be willing to allow me to 'withdraw for revision and let that be known to the Press saying that he himself has become dissatisfied and had written to ask it back'. This to save my dignity and to deliver me from the curse of the Abbey's rejection when dealing with an English Manager. If W.B. Yeats had known me as faintly as he thinks he knows me well, he wouldn't have wasted his time – and mine – making such a suggestion. I am too big for this sort of mean and petty shuffling, this lousy perversion of the truth. There is going to be no damned secrecy with me surrounding the Abbey's rejection of the play. Does he think that I would practice in my life the prevarication and wretchedness that I laugh at in my plays?

O'Casey, letter to Lennox Robinson, 2 May 1928

[The full correspondence is printed in *The Letters of Sean O'Casey, Volume 1, 1910-1941*, p. 265-76. Yeats's rejection of the play ended O'Casey's close working association with the Abbey: it lost a playwright and O'Casey lost a theatre. *The Silver Tassie* thus became the first of O'Casey's plays to be published before it received a production – a pattern which was to continue throughout his life and a situation which, as an experimental playwright, he was to find frustrating and inhibiting. Eventually the impresario C.B. Cochran agreed to put on the play in London. Raymond Massey was invited to direct it, and describes the experience in his autobiography *A Hundred Different Lives*.]

Cochran's production of *The Silver Tassie* . . . was of the utmost significance for Sean. He was desperately anxious to vindicate his work of the shame of rejection. But he knew the *Tassie* was open to adverse criticism, that he had broken some of the traditional rules of dramaturgy, that he had completely altered mood and style with his symbolic and satirical second act, and had ignored continuity and convention. Before we started rehearsals he said to me with a twinkle in those poor, weak eyes, 'I can be of no help to you with the second act, but I do believe that the play will act well when you get it on its feet'. He was right. With the aid of an inspired cast and contributions from several talents in the art world, *The Silver Tassie* achieved a triumph at its opening. . . . George Bernard Shaw summed it up in his tribute to a fellow Irishman, 'It's a hell of a play!' he shouted as he stood with cheering first-nighters.

Raymond Massey,
letter to *The Sean O'Casey Review*, IV 2 (1978)

It is a difficult play . . . because in one of the scenes I have attempted something which has never been done on the stage before. One of Mr. Yeats's objections to the play was that it contained no dominating character, and for that reason I feel it is a better play than *Juno and the Paycock* (which is the poorest thing I have had produced) and *The Plough and the Stars*. In *Tassie* the tragedy dominates the characters.

O'Casey, interviewed in *The Observer*, 6 Oct. 1929

Many years may pass before Mr. O'Casey's art ceases to produce confusion in the mind of an audience accustomed by long theatrical usage to consistency of mood. Hitherto it has commonly been demanded of a play that it be tragic, or that it be comic, or, if by profession a tragi-comedy, that the forms contrasted should remain distinct, the one appearing as a 'relief' to the other. This theory Mr. O'Casey has definitely abandoned, and has substituted for it another, still very unfamiliar in the theatre. . . . We are no longer invited to give attention to one aspect of life and to consider it dominant for the time being. The unity of the work of art is no longer to depend upon the consistency of its material. Instead, as if the drama were being rolled over and tossed in air before our eyes like a diamond, we are so to observe its facets of tragedy, comedy, and open farce that their flashing becomes at last one flash and perhaps, by imaginative and symbolic transition, one spiritual light. . . .

Of even greater value is his attempt to break free from the bonds of naturalism by the bold use of verse. Anyone in this history of a footballer who was maimed in the War may break into verse at any moment. A group of soldiers, resting at night from their labours, falls into a rhythmical chanting which has no relation with the matter or manner of everyday speech. Another group joins them, and all, falling upon their knees, send up a bitter prayer to a gun raised against the skyline. Above them, like the figure of Death itself, crouches the solitary figure of a man, chanting . . . a terrible parody of the Valley of Dry Bones. The whole scene is almost a masterpiece. Mr. Augustus John's setting is its background. Mr. Raymond Massey's direction of the stage – his assembling of the soldiers in closely packed groups and his disposition of them so that they have continuously the quality of great sculpture – marks him as a producer who is also a poet.

Mr. O'Casey's attempt to make his play take wings from naturalistic earth succeeds; we move in a new plane of imagination. Yet the scene is not a masterpiece. The elements are not truly compounded. . . . The greater part of its effect springs from its setting, the leaning crucifix, the shadowy gun, the grouping of men, and the rhythm of language – the rythym of language, not the substance of it. Though the use of poetry has lifted the play from earth to dream, the poetry itself has not force enough to sustain so great a suspense. . . .

The other acts are more limited in their range. They are not as the second act is, a brilliant failure that might have been the core of a masterpiece. But in them also Mr. O'Casey is working at his proper experiment, twirling his diamond, leaping suddenly from a music-hall turn at a telephone to a transcendental dialogue between a blind man and a cripple, giving to a dance at a football club an extraordinary tragic significance, matching a poem with a waltz, wringing a new intensity from a scene in a hospital ward. . . .

Charles Morgan, *The Times*, 12 Oct. 1929

Basically Yeats was right. *The Silver Tassie* is a bad play. It contains hunks of powerful, top-grade O'Casey, and even at its worst fails on a grand scale. But it does not hang together, never achieves the fusion of particular pain and epic pity it aims at. . . . One can see O'Casey's need to let the vitality of the first act trickle away in futility and cynicism. But the last half of the play loses pace and organization as well. The trouble is the attempt to return to such a level from the abstraction of the second, expressionist act. . . . This, the bone which stuck in the throat of the Abbey and later Irish audiences, is a remarkable piece of theatre. . . . Written a year after *Journey's End* it's as timeless as *Oh! What a Lovely War!* In it, you can see the later O'Casey emerging. The rest of the play crumbles round it like a pallid, disintegrating chrysalis. . . . Like its hero, *The Silver Tassie* is a torso: massive, honourable but only half alive.

Ronald Bryden, *The Observer*, 14 Sept. 1969

Sean O'Casey's rarely performed post-mortem on the First World War . . . gets a distinguished, memorable revival at the Aldwych. The strange, seemingly self-contained second act is rightly conceived as the core of the play. Set on the borders of an anonymous battlefield, it is redolent with pain and brutality – yet this is made physically bearable by the transfiguring of the wearied and wounded soldiers into chanters of a sort of militarized plain-song. They are, as it were, inheritors of the devastated monastery in which they now find themselves feeling towards a liturgy to ritualize the raw horrors of the trenches. David Jones directs this act magnificently, blunting neither the exposed edges of its suffering nor the terrible pathos of its poetry: and John Bury blends design and lighting into a lowering, nightmarish landscape of crumbling arches and twilit distances.

This sequence is, admittedly, a director's dream, and in some ways the domestic scenes which hem it in – a prelude and aftermath to the maiming of one manhood – are so much more difficult as they are less immediately impressive . . . but generally the transition from the homely naturalism of the first act across the chasm of war into the slightly dazed, emotionally diminished atmosphere of the third and fourth is tactfully, purposefully realized. Or maybe one should call them movements rather than acts – movements in a sombre, inhuman symphony that remains unfinished.

Simon Trussler, *Tribune*, 26 Sept. 1969

Famous as the cause of O'Casey's self-imposed exile from Dublin, the play . . . is still hardly known in the theatre: and David Jones's excellent production is one of the most rewarding exhumations I can remember. It shows a dramatist of immense natural gifts and past attainment extending himself into new and difficult territory. . . . In spite of its celebrated second act . . . *The Silver Tassie* is not really a war play. It is about the aftermath of adventure, and the ease with which the healthy reject the maimed, and edit them into oblivion for their own peace of mind. The girls take new men: the old men still sing, 'Let me like a soldier fall': all blinder than the man who lost his eyes at the front.

John Bury's designs underline this point by using the same material for battledress and domestic furnishings: as do performances like Helen Mirren's Susie and Bruce Myer's Barney by making a virtue of discontinuity of character.

Irving Wardle, *The Times*, 11 Sept. 1969

Whatever one's reaction to *The Silver Tassie*, no one who is deeply interested in the theatre will dispute the validity of Sean O'Casey's final comment on the rejection of his play: 'Dramatists cannot go on imitating themselves, and when they get tired of that, imitating others. They must change, must experiment, must develop their power, or try to, if the drama is to live.' Brecht would have agreed with that; and so, too, would the seemingly placid Lady Gregory who as long ago as 1914 had written: 'The desire to experiment is like fire in the blood.' This possibly was the reason why, of the three directors concerned, she was waveringly on the side of the rejected playwright. But for Sean O'Casey and the Abbey Theatre, things were never quite the same again.

Gabriel Fallon,
programme note to the Abbey Theatre revival, 1972

Within the Gates

'A Play of Four Scenes in a London Park'.
Written: 1928-33.
First performed: Royalty Th., London, 7 Feb. 1934 (dir. and
    des. Norman MacDermott; music by Herbert Hughes).
Revived: National Th., New York, 22 Oct. 1934 (dir. Melvyn
    Douglas; des. James Reynolds; music by Milton Lusk; with
    Lillian Gish as the Young Whore); Lyric Th., Belfast, 6 Mar.
    1974 (dir. Jim Sheridan).
Published: London: Macmillan, 1933; 'stage version' in
    Collected Plays, II; in *Selected Plays*; in *The Sean O'Casey
    Reader*; and in *Complete Plays 2*. (The 'stage version' was the
    result of extensive revision of the text by O'Casey after the
    play was produced in London and New York.)
Translated into: German.

---

*Set in Hyde Park during the Depression, the action, divided into
four scenes, encompasses the seasonal and daily cycles – spring
(morning), summer (noon), autumn (evening), winter (night).
Symbolic characters representing a cross section of society pass
through the Park providing a human backcloth for the central
conflict which concerns a young whore, who is dying of a heart
condition. Her soul is fought over by The Dreamer (a poet), The
Atheist, The Bishop (her father), and The Salvation Army
Officer, each believing that their 'faith' is the only means of
salvation. Although she dies making the sign of the cross it is
The Dreamer's humanist vision which stays with her.*

[O'Casey originally planned 'a film of Hyde Park, London, its life, its
pathos, its pattern; its meaning to the rest of England'. He put the idea
to Alfred Hitchcock who, although initially enthusiastic, did not
pursue it. (A rough draft of the scenario is in the Berg Collection,
New York Public Library.) O'Casey turned the film into a play,
which he finished in July 1933.]

I am working hard towards the completion of my new play, *Within
the Gates*. It is the hardest job that I have ever attempted, making me
exclaim with Yeats, 'my curse on plays that have to be set up in fifty
ways!' . . . There will be music, songs sung singly and in chorus, and
though the work may not be a great one, or even fine, I'm sure it will

41

be interesting.

O'Casey, letter to George Jean Nathan, May 1933
reprinted in *Letters, 1*, p. 457

The treatment being plotless, and impressionistic, with mass recitatives, dance, and groupings, is that of an impatient rebel, savagely debunking life, including debunkers themselves; but however impressive, I suggest that it weakens the theme.

If his characters were speaking instead of O'Casey, it would be less irritating to the average theatre audience, who will certainly regard his method as pretentious; and would lend force to his ever-present message that starving men and women cannot be fobbed off with dogmas of any kind.

P.L.M., *Daily Herald*, 8 Feb. 1934

Mr. O'Casey is struggling towards a new mode of expression (or, more accurately, an old and forgotten one), and his play is not for those who want an ordinary 'show'. It is for those who view the theatre more widely and courageously. Least of all in the theatre, where so many elements go to the total effect, is the way of experiment easy. Honourable it certainly is, and exciting for those who are fascinated by theatrical technique, but easy, never. Mr. O'Casey, in revolt against the realistic routine of our time, has gone a long way further than he did in *The Silver Tassie* towards a theatre of poetic power as well as prosaic fun.

Ivor Brown, *The Observer*, 11 Feb. 1934

[Gordon Beckles in the *Daily Express*, 8 Feb., stated categorically, 'It is not a play'; and James Agate in the *Sunday Times*, 11 Feb., declared it to be 'pretentious rubbish'. Both reviews, together with O'Casey's rejoinders are reprinted in *The Letters of Sean O'Casey, Volume 1*, p. 491-502.]

The more [the experimental playwright] tried to put into a play the less chance he'd have of a production in England, so he had to decide whether he would model a play so as to squeeze it towards triviality, or persist in experimental imagination, and suffer for it. On the other hand, if he did get a production of an experimental play, he would be forced to submit to a rag-and-tag one, one that would be cheapened so much that half the life would be gutted out of it. The English critic, by and large, would measure the play by its furtive, underhand performance, so giving the play no chance of a better and deserving production in the future.

O'Casey, *Rose and Crown*, p. 130–1

[The problem of the playwright without a theatre within which to practice was one which, for O'Casey, remained unresolved, but as far as *Within the Gates* was concerned, the failure of the play in London did not impede plans for the New York premiere.]

When the text of *Within the Gates* was published last year, it seemed to many of us that Mr. O'Casey . . . had overreached himself in a poetic medium beyond his strength. But out of the dead print of the text a glorious drama rose last evening with songs and dances, with colours and lights, with magnificent lines that cried out for noble speaking. For Mr. O'Casey is right. He knows that the popular theatre has withered, and he also has the gift to redeem it with a drama that sweeps along through the loves and terrors of mankind. . . .

Being the theatre of spiritual magnificence, it needs all the glories of stage art, and it has them in this superb production. Last year *Within the Gates* was drably produced in London. Here George Bushar and John Tuerk, . . . have given it a memorable production, directed with rare sensibility by Melvyn Douglas. The incidental music . . . enkindles the drama as much as anything Mr. O'Casey has written. The songs have a purity of meaning; the chant for the down-and-outs is macabre. . . . The designer of the setting and costumes has understood the problem of fantasy in all its ramifications, and endowed *Within the Gates* with a decor that lifts it into visual eminence. . . .

As the tortured young woman, Lillian Gish gives a performance instinct with the spirit of the drama. Never did an actress play a part with more sincerity or deeper comprehension. . . . Mr. O'Casey has written a great play. There is iron in its bones and blood in its veins and lustre in its flesh, and its feet rest on the good brown earth.

Brooks Atkinson, *New York Times*, 23 Oct. 1934

As it is produced in the New York theatre, with the lavish talents of an unusually fine company devoted to its performance, it comes out as a moving drama, with 'simple austerity, swinging merriment, beauty in music of word and colour of scene, and (almost, but not quite) with a tragedy too deep for tears'. Those are the qualities that Mr. O'Casey desires to bring back to the theatre, according to his own words in an interview he gave to the *New York Times* before the play opened. Those are, indeed, the qualities inherent in the best lines and scenes of *Within the Gates*. Seeing it performed is a rich theatre experience.

Edith J.R. Isaacs, *Theatre Arts Monthly*, Dec. 1934

To Mr. O'Casey this play may be 'a religious function', but to most of us it will be rather a hedonistic farrago, beautifully written in spots, formless and pretentious, a symbol which its author never intended – a symbol of confusion at once moral and aesthetic which permeates so much of modern writing. In short, Mr. O'Casey's poetry has gone to his head and obscured many things, among them dramatic unity, good taste, sound philosophy and common sense. In abandoning his native Ireland he has pulled up his roots, and without roots poetic imagination soon becomes a dry and sterile thing.

Grenville Vernon, *The Commonweal*, 9 Nov. 1934

[Despite the mixed critical reception, the public responded positively and the play ran for 101 performances. A tour was planned of thirteen cities, but while the production was playing in Philadelphia, the Mayor of Boston sought to ban the performances planned for his city. The Board of Censorship in Boston upheld the Mayor's moral and religious objections to the play and the tour was abandoned. The play did not receive a professional production in Ireland until 1974 – at the Lyric Theatre in Belfast, whose declared policy it is to present in time all O'Casey's plays.]

It's not vintage O'Casey – here he turns from naturalism to expressionistic techniques that are not always successful – but with his sharp insight he laughs at humanity's follies and grieves over the sad agony of man's fate.

Gerard McCreesh, *Sunday Independent*, Dublin, 10 Mar. 1974

Within the Gates ... may not be one of the Lyric's most exciting productions, but it is certainly one of its most moving and colourful performances. ... It is really a morality play, with O'Casey making the best possible use of symbolism, poetry, song, and dance.

Irish News, (Belfast), 9 Mar. 1974

The End of the Beginning

'A Comedy in One Act'.

Written: *c*. 1932.

First performed: Abbey Th., Dublin, 8 Feb. 1937 (dir. Arthur Shields; with F.J. McCormick as Barry Derrill and P.J. Carolan as Darry Berrill).

Revived: 'Q' Th., London, 16 Oct. 1939 (dir. Beatrix Lehmann); Unity Th., London, 22 May 1953 (dir. David Dawson); Forum-Theater, Berlin, 8 Aug., 1966 (dir. Moritz Milar); Volksbühne, Berlin, 1967 (dir. Klaus Tews); Théâtre de Bourgogne, France, 1968; Nameless Th., New York, 17 Mar. 1976 (dir. Arthur Kirson); Schaubühne am Halleschen Ufer, Berlin, 15 Mar. 1975 (dir. the actors); Theater der Stadt Brandenburg, 1976 (dir. Gerhard Wruck).

Published: in (*Windfalls* London: Macmillan, 1934); in *Collected Plays I*; in *Five One-Act Plays*; and in *Complete Plays 1*. *Translated into*: French, German, Persian, Romanian, Russian, Spanish.

It is an old tale – that of the man who thought woman's work trivial and easy – and one that lends itself readily to farcical treatment on the stage. In this little play Darry Berrill thinks he can do the housework better and faster than his wife, so they exchange jobs for a while. Darry might have been a success in the home had there been no distracting influence; but what with his 'physical jerks' and his mandoline the home lacked fascination. He did his exercises on the floor to the music of a gramophone; sang his song with Barry Derrill to the accompaniment of two mandolines and much laughter from the audience; fooled about with an alarm clock, the domestic crockery, the pig food, the electric light, and an oil drum, and reached the climax of folly by tethering the cow to a chair by a rope passed down the chimney. When the cow became too restive and Barry Derrill loosed his hold, Darry Berrill went up the chimney at the end of the rope, but came crashing down again when the wife released the rope from the cow outside.

Its all good, plain foolery, without particular meaning or individual distinction; it might have been written by the rawest novice to the ranks of the playwrights. It is sheer farce, without characterization other than that imparted by excellent acting, and its situations

45

are purely conventional. The artistry of Sean O'Casey is missing, but a brighter and sunnier disposition is discovered in the playwright.

The Irish Times, 9 Feb. 1937

[Based on a folk tale, this play was written, together with *A Pound on Demand* (see below) as a music-hall sketch for Arthur Sinclair, but unperformed until a first-rate Abbey cast took it up five years later.]

The End of the Beginning, in spirit a music-hall sketch, is based on the notion common to most men that housework is so easy that any man could do it 'on his head' so to speak, and have time to spare for all manner of diversions. The fallaciousness of this notion is worked out in a way which shows that the author shares with Mr. Shaw a relish for knockabout farce. So, luckily, do Mr. Edgar K. Bruce and Mr. John Laurie who, in Laurel and Hardy parts, raise the whole thing to a high pitch of physical ingenuity.

The Times, 17 Oct. 1939

Mr. O'Casey is evidently also a master of pure farce, and the calamities that crowd upon the mistaken husband . . . when he invites the help of a short-sighted friend . . . migh arouse the envy of old hands at writing Aldwych farces.

The Times, 23 May 1953

A Pound on Demand

'A Sketch in One Act'.
Written: *c*. 1932.
First performed: 'Q' Th., London, 16 Oct. 1939 (dir. Beatrix
    Lehmann; with Irene Handl as the Girl and John Laurie
    as Jerry).
Revived: International Th., New York, 19 Dec. 1946 (dir. Victor
    Jory); Mercury Th., 18 Sept. 1947 (dir. Denis Carey);
    Theatre Guild, Playhouse Th., New York, 15 Apr. 1959 (dir.
    Hume Cronyn); Kammerspiele des Deutschen Theaters,
    Berlin, 6 Oct. 1965 (dir. Adolf Dresen); Mermaid Th.,
    London, Apr. 1967 (dir. Jack MacGowran, who also played
    Jerry; with Shivaun O'Casey as the Girl); Théâtre National de
    Strasbourg, Mar. 1978 (dir. Jean-Pierre Vincent).

Published: in *Windfalls*; in *Collected Plays I*; in *Five One-Act Plays*; and in *Complete Plays 1*. *Translated into*: Afrikaans, French, German, Irish, Russian, Spanish.

Its farcical situation is adroitly transformed into comedy. Yet all it depicts is the unavailing attempt of two workmen, one more inebriated than the other, to withdraw a pound from the Savings Bank at a Post Office.

The Times, 17 Oct. 1939

[Like *The End of the Beginning* (see p. 45), this was written as a music-hall sketch, but went unperformed professionally until 1939. Jack MacGowran later directed it as a 'curtain-raiser' to *Gunman* at the Mermaid Theatre.]

Jack MacGowran is a pipe-cleaner man uneasily in charge of a bottle-stopper head several times too large for his endlessly bendable limbs. . . . He is an actor designed by nature to cartoon the perpetual under-dog (or perhaps under-mouse), the poor, wee, timorous, cowering beastie under the floor-boards of society who yet survives at all attempts to trap or poison him. In Beckett or O'Casey, both in their way Irish poets of poverty, he embodies brilliantly the heroic pessimism of the born survivor whose only ambition in a disintegrating world is to exist for just one more day. As the drunken applicant at the Post Office counter, manhandled by his sober mate with as little ceremony as the lizard juror in *Alice in Wonderland* and almost equally bemused by the bureaucratic formalities, Mr. MacGowran seems to me to challenge Chaplin. He is reduced simply to a casing for alcohol, a human bottle on shuddering legs, for whom the movement of a single muscle requires a titanic battle between opposing forces.

Alan Brien, *Sunday Telegraph*, 9 Apr. 1967

A mad, mad world with a shaggy, slovenly and bewildered post-office girl awkwardly handling bits of string, scissors, and glue and constantly dropping things. A perfect pictorial expression of a non-technical world of dreamers and odd-jobbers, of the fundamental mess of things. The end of the play is a masterpiece of stagecraft with the ultimate revolt of the two drunkards that raise their clenched fists

at bureaucracy as fantastic submachine-guns can be heard outside
while hundreds of empty plastic bottles suddenly shower down on
them from the rigging-loft and engulf them on a jig-tune.

Emile Jean Dumay, on the Strasbourg production,
The Sean O'Casey Review, V, 1 (Fall 1978)

The Star Turns Red

Play in four acts.
Written: 1938-39.
First performed: Unity Th., London, 12 Mar. 1940 (dir. John
Allen; des. Lawrence Gowing; music by Alan Bush).
Revived: Unity Th., 24 July 1946 (dir. Ted Willis); Théâtre de
Commune d'Aubervilliers, Théâtre Recamier, Paris, Oct. 1962
(dir. Gabriel Garran); Maxim Gorki Theater, Berlin, 2 Nov.
1968 (dir. Kurt Veth); Abbey Th., Dublin, 2 Feb. 1978 (dir.
Tomas MacAnna).
Published: London: Macmillan, 1940; in *Collected Plays II*; and
in *Complete Plays 2*. *Translated into*: Chinese, French,
German, Hungarian, Russian.

*At Christmas time 'To-morrow or the next day' a strike led by
Red Jim and his communist Red Guards results in a bitter and
bloody confrontation with the fascist Saffron Shirts supported
by the Catholic Christian Front, led by the Purple Priest. The
conflict between Communism and Fascism is depicted through
Red Jim's struggle against State, Church, and his own Union –
whose unscrupulous leaders, controlled by the Purple Priest,
seek to betray him and sabotage the strike – and the story of two
brothers, Jack and Kian, who fight on opposing sides. Jack's
belief in Communism is shared by his girlfriend, Julia, and her
father, Michael, but both men die in the struggle, Michael shot
by Kian as he attempts to rescue Julia from a whipping by the
Saffron Shirts. As Jack dies in the climactic battle, Kian and the
Brown Priest, sympathetic to the workers, defy the Purple Priest
and remain with Jack's body; the soldiers cross the barricades
and join the Red Guards; and to symbolize the possibility of a
successful workers' revolution, the Christmas star turns red.*

[In a letter to Lennox Robinson, 9 Feb. 1922, O'Casey wrote that he 'was thinking of writing a play around Jim Larkin – The Red Star – in which he would never appear though (be) responsible for all the action'. It was, however, to be another sixteen years before he wrote the play, with 'Red Jim' now as a central character.]

I hope you'll see something in it. As well as being something of a confession of faith, it is, I think, a play; and, possibly, the best of its kind which has been written – which isn't saying a lot. There are, anyhow, some good lines in it. It is, I think, much more compact than *Within The Gates*, though I don't yet know just how much of the verse form ought to go to a play dealing with present-day life. There was too much singing in *Within The Gates*, or, maybe, as is most probable, the singing was in the wrong place; or the chanting, or whatever we can call it. The action takes place during the last few hours of a Christmas Eve; and by this means, I've managed, I think, to give an ironical twist here and there. And I've tried to give a symbolism in the colouring of the four scenes, as you will see.

O'Casey, letter to George Jean Nathan, 8 Feb. 1939

[The play was published by Macmillan in London a month before the first production, but the New York branch of the company decided against publication.]

Not only do I feel that the publication of this play in America at this time would do you immeasurable damage, but by the same token it would damage us too. America is rabid against Communism, and I should hate to see the book brought out over your name now because I feel that it would be a sure way of alienating your friends among the readers in this country. This would hurt us too, because if, as I hope, we are to have the pleasure of publishing for you for years to come, I fear that publication of *The Star Turns Red* would make our road a difficult one in so far as your books are concerned for the future, at least for the immediate future.

Letter to O'Casey from George P. Brett, Jr., 16 Feb. 1940

[O'Casey described the play as 'a warning' and one that 'plunges into the turmoil between the Fascists, a Church with her eyes on the earth; and the trumpet-call claims of the militant workers.' He corresponded from Devon with the leading contributors to the Unity Theatre

49

production, and reveals his concern with the visual aspects of the presentation. He found the idea of the Clenched-Fist on the drop-curtain too overt: 'If a curtain is to symbolize the play, I suggested it should have on it, a huge church; a huge factory chimney; a long vista of tiny houses; a star in the sky; and behind the star, a "cloud no bigger than a man's hand" – see Bible – showing the form, in a cloudy way, of a clenched fist . . .'. He told John Allen, the director, that he had conceived the scene (the family home) as a 'cubic black coffin in which the people lived; touched by the Church spire and the Factory chimney; and the sky with a star in it . . .'. However, having seen Lawrence Gowing's designs he realized: 'With the whole conception of the play, the closed-in coffin-room won't do. The influence the Spire, the Chimney, and the Star were to have would then be lost. I forgot these, till Lawrence Gowing reminded me of them; and also of the mingling of "realism" and symbolism in the play, suggesting the same thing in the designs. I agree with him. And I think, and so does Eileen, that he has cleverly done this in his designs. I like them very much; and I don't see how they can be bettered for the purposes of the play; unless we had a big theatre and a bigger purse: two things that might ruin the play and the production.' See letters to Peter Newmark, 31 Jan. and 7 Feb. 1940, in *The Letters of Sean O'Casey, Volume 1*, p. 840, 843.]

Mr. O'Casey's play is a masterpiece. . . . The passion, pathos, humour, and above all, poetry . . . are there for all the world to see and hear. . . . Further to be advanced on this play's behalf are its drive, its variety, . . . its perfect setting in the Ireland of 'to-day or to-morrow'. I find the piece to be a *magnum opus* of compassion *and* a revolutionary work. I see in it a flame of propaganda tempered to the condition of dramatic art, as an Elizabethan understood that art. To one such a proud prelate was a prelate whose pride was whole and absolute, and free of those erosions and nibblings insisted on by an age which realizes that nothing is whole and absolute. That is why the Red Priest in this play is more than a whole-hogger for things as they are; he is a medieval whole-hogger. . . .

Opposite, as the films have it, to the Red Priest is the people's leader, Red Jim, who is as much a model of Communist virtue as, let us say, Shakespeare's Henry V was a model of manly excellence. And, of course, Priest and Leader go to it hammer-and-tongs, like those English and French armies. . . . One side says 'Ding', and the other 'Dong'. And that is all there is to it, excepting, possibly, the Brown Priest who, as the spirit of compromise, tries to ding and dong together by saying 'Dell'! Let me insist on this play's Elizabethan quality. No Shavian nonsense here, whereby the protagonists, in this case meaning antagonists, put their knees under the mahogany and obligingly put each other's cases!

In the first act a Saffron-Shirted Fascist shoots a Worker whose Communist daughter the Red Priest has ordered to be whipped. In the second act a Worker beats up half-a-dozen corrupt trades union leaders. Let those who blame the Unity Theatre audience for vocalizing their delight at this ask themselves how an Elizabethan audience took Fluellen's beating up of Pistol, and Pistol's beating up of the French soldier. The third act, which begins with the halt and the blind, the phthisic, and the deformed processing round the dead man's bier, is, pictorially speaking, sheer Webster, though exactly what the mourners stand for is a little baffling. For while these are the victims of poverty, they are not proposing to do anything about it. . . . After the procession the two sides square up to each other over the coffin, the Priest deploying all his powers of rhetoric and casuistry against the lava-like flow of the leader's impassioned oratory, whose speciousness is at once innocent and over-riding.

Then follows the fourth and weakest act. . . . There is an alleged comic scene between two workmen . . . [and] the play concludes with the seige of the Workers by the military and the police, done in dumb-show, and a sudden change of heart on the part of these two bodies. During this the Star, coldly glittering from the beginning, now turns red. . . . I came away impressed above all by a verbal splendour . . . at last, Mr. O'Casey has achieved that towards which in *The Silver Tassie* and *Within the Gates* he was feeling his way.

James Agate, *Sunday Times*, 17 Mar. 1940

The Star Turns Red is a play with characters who exist only as symbols to expound a morality. Three views of life are represented by three sets of human symbols – the Catholic, the Fascist and the Communist. Mr. O'Casey – who seems to have but a faltering hold on the implications of social ideas – sympathizes most with the Communist and understands best the Catholic. More than any other of his plays, this one is saturated with Catholic ideas and Catholic imagery. It is the Star of Bethlehem that turns an embarrassed pink in the last act of Revolutionary triumph produced perhaps by a wave of the wand from the Unity Theatre's famous Fairy Wish-fulfilment. . . . Mr. O'Casey is not a Communist at all really, but a Christian Socialist who hates the Church because it has not given the poor the equality which Christ and the Brown Priest of his play represent for him. . . .

It is implied that the young Communist hero and heroine are the only people in the play (which represents the whole of Dublin) who enjoy a really satisfactory sexual relationship. Thus Communism is Life and everything else is a perversion of life leading towards death. Nevertheless, his portraits of Communists are unconvincing in the manner of those paintings of young people in the art galleries of Moscow and Berlin, marching towards a goal. Their faces are flushed and healthy, but the spectator is left with an uneasy question on his lips: 'Well what are you going to do when you get there?' The answer is of course 'Build', to be followed by pictures and plays about people building.

Sean O'Casey has a great gift of language and this play, even if it is a failure, must be of interest to everyone who cares for the serious drama. It is always well written, and the handling of large numbers of characters is skilful. Yet it suffers from the disadvantage that all the characters are 'types' in the sense that they are labelled and numbered and fit into the Communist scheme of morality which . . . grades people according to their usefulness to a cause. . . . The play is a virtuous exercise but it succeeds best where Sean O'Casey shows obvious failure to be a good Party Member.

Stephen Spender, *New Statesman*, 16 Mar. 1940

MacAnna's direction was . . . superb, and some scenes remain extraordinarily vivid: the memory-jarring entrance of the Saffron Shirts to the sound of Hitler-era martial music, and the contrasting joyful first appearance of the Red Guards, marching down the aisles, carrying torches, singing and challenging the Saffron Shirts. For sheer terror, nothing could match the appearance of the Purple Priest in the first act. A huge 'Flash in the Circle' (which, inverted, spelled out 'SS') was projected onto the backdrop and the powerful sounds of an organ medley swirled through the theatre. The priest, played by Patrick Laffan, appeared, wearing regal purple satin, carrying a crozier, and surrounded by a coterie of Saffron Shirts and other priests. Less frightening but no less vivid was the funeral scene of Michael, his coffin being carried out by the Red Guards to a mournful song. The scene was in the third act, considered by O'Casey to be the finest act he ever wrote, bar the second act of the *Tassie*.

Robert G. Lowery, *Sean O'Casey Review*, IV, 2 (Spring 1978)

Purple Dust

'A Wayward Comedy in Three Acts'.
Written: 1939-1940.
First performed: People's Th., Newcastle-upon-Tyne, 16 Dec. 1943 (dir. Peter Trower).

Revived: Old Vic Company, Liverpool Playhouse, 31 Oct. 1945
(first professional production; dir. Eric Capon, des. Kathleen
Ankers); Cherry Lane Th., New York, 27 Dec. 1956 (dir.
Philip Burton); Mermaid Th., London, 15 Aug. 1962 (dir.
Peter Duguid); Théâtre de la Cité, Villeurbanne, 1965 (dir.
J. Rosner); Berliner Ensemble, 14 Feb. 1966 (dir. Hans-
Georg Simmgen; des. Andreas Reinhardt); Lyric Th., Belfast,
28 Mar. 1973 (dir. Tomas MacAnna); Abbey Th., Dublin,
30 Jan. 1975 (dir. Tomas MacAnna; des. Brian Collins);
Hissisches Staatstheater, Wiesbaden, 26 Nov. 1978.
Published: London: Macmillan, 1940; in *Collected Plays III*; in
Selected Plays; in *Genius of the Irish Theatre* (New York:
New American Library, 1960); in *Three More Plays*; in *The
Sean O'Casey Reader*; in *Six Plays*; and in *Complete Plays 3*.
Translated into: Chinese, Czech, French, German,
Hungarian, Italian, Japanese, Persian, Russian.

*In a bizarre attempt to revive the aristocratic and pastoral life of
rural Ireland, two wealthy Englishmen – Cyril Poges, a
stockbroker, and Basil Stoke, a scholar – acquire an old Tudor
mansion, to which they bring their respective mistresses,
Souhaun and Avril, hiring a group of assorted Irish workmen to
restore it to its former glory. The Englishmen plan to return to
nature, thus evading the Second World War in neutral Ireland
while protecting their capitalist interest in England; but they are
thwarted by two of the workmen, O'Killigain, a revolutionary,
and O'Dempsey, a visionary, who charm Avril and Souhaun
and eventually carry them off; by the ineptitude of the other
workmen; by the unpredictability of the local amenities; and
finally by the weather: as the storm rages, a strange figure
appears, representing the spirit of the rising river, and threatens
to sweep the house and its inhabitants away.*

I think it is, in some ways, an odd play. . . . At first it was to be just a
skit on the country; but it changed a little into, maybe, a kind of an
allegorical form. The idea crept into my head after a visit to a family
living in a Tudor House here; suffering all kinds of inconveniences
because of its age and history; going about with lanterns, and eating
in semi-gloom. Terrible torture for the sake of a tumbledown house

with a name! I've never gone there since. I was perished with the cold, and damaged with the gloom. However, you'll read the play; and of course, I hope you'll find something in it. A lot of the humour is, I think, pretty broad, and a little exaggerated, but we Irish are fond of adding to things.

O'Casey, letter to George Jean Nathan, 14 Feb. 1940

[In 1953 Sam Wanamaker, the American actor and director, set up a production, in which O'Casey was actively involved, which toured the North of England and reached the Theatre Royal, Glasgow, towards the end of April.]

Purple Dust ... shows – for those who might otherwise think it curious – why O'Casey's reputation can survive silence or even worse. He certainly contributes an uncommon vitality to the revolt against realism. If it were possible to have a passionate, philosophical farce, with music, based on a single wise joke, then the extraordinary creation might be thought successful. Calling itself a 'wayward comedy', it blows in your eye as blithely, and as irritatingly, as a row of Glasgow chimneys in an Atlantic gale. ... It is in part as if Ben Travers had kissed the Blarney, in part like a slightly intoxicated light opera, and in part like a sort of Moonshine Boulevard. Miles Malleson and Walter Hudd – recognizable Englishmen in a cast bristling with London Irish names – have taken a wonderfully doddering Irish castle and are trying, it seems, to recover a false golden age in the teeth of the gales and the shrewd, proud gibes of the surrounding natives. ... Mr. O'Casey has included a good deal of song and dance, and the opening chorus, with Mr. Malleson and most of the company prancing round the stage in smocks, is more than a little alarming. But we quickly learn to expect anything, including a cow in the mouldering Great Hall, a man with a yellow beard who from time to time pokes his head through a jagged hole in the ceiling, and a blasted rowan tree as tragic relief. There is a deal of fine, ranting language – more resembling prose that sounds like verse than verse that sounds like prose, which is a pleasant change from the run of anti-realist plays.

Manchester Guardian, 29 Apr. 1953

There are no politics as such in this play; its foundation, its roof, floor, windows, and doors are built out of laughter. ... The play isn't an attack on England, not even on any particular class in the country.

... It is to some extent, a symbolic play, and unconsciously, a prophetic one too. The auld hoose, beloved by so many for so long, is in a bad way; old things are passing away, and new things are appearing in the sky, on the horizon, and right here in the middle of us. The house is falling, and we hardly know where to start to pick up the bits. . . . Within the symbol and the prophecy is woven slapstick and rhythm, a song here, a little dance there, some comic manners of man.

O'Casey, *New York Herald Tribune*, 23 Dec. 1956

Anyone looking for the absolute boundaries of the theatre can have them now any old night. To catch drama at its loosest, sloppiest, and in a certain sense liveliest, one has only to grab a cab and head way downtown to Commerce Street and the Cherry Lane Theatre. There, against a splendidly microscopic setting that seems to stretch to infinity, Sean O'Casey's eighteen-year-old comic broadside *Purple Dust* is being splattered with furious and foolish gusto all over the premises. . . . As the rattle-tongued Mr. O'Casey spills out his run-on tale of a couple of Englishmen who are determined to restore ancient, aristocratic ways to Ireland, he doesn't hesitate to interrupt the beginning exposition with a bar to two of song or a real bout of barn dancing. Heels go high in the air before we are quite sure what the revel is about. . . .

Faults will be obvious as this out-of-control roller-coaster careens into space. In toying around with spotlighted symbols, O'Casey is himself guilty of killing primroses. In letting his structure go any old way his lightning-quick mind happens to veer at the moment, the values of orderly progression and dramatic suspense and even simple coherence are lost. . . . But something is left: the wild, and now and then wonderful, drunken improvisation in which all drama began, the disorderly conduct that has been known to end in art, the heedless and headstrong exuberance of a Saturday-night jig in a borrowed stable. *Purple Dust* may arrive at formlessness rather than the new and ranging form it aspires to; but it's pretty much what you'd expect a careless saturnalia to be – random, rowdy, fun.

Walter Kerr, *New York Herald Tribune*, 6 Jan. 1957

The symbolism is crass . . . and the basic joke is hollow: what bores one about the English upper classes is not, as O'Casey insists, that they are ignorant of country life, but that they know it inside out and never stop talking about it.

Kenneth Tynan, *The Observer*, 19 Aug. 1962

O'Casey . . . is a man of principle who likes men and women. It is an uncomfortable combination for a dramatist who believes in revolution. How can one condemn to destruction, ruin, and spoilation people in whose eccentricities one delights? But Mr. O'Casey is driven by his convictions to attempt, in *Purple Dust*, this impossible and, dramatically speaking, suicidal task. His sombre and imperial title shows the habit of his mind: to O'Casey the thinker, statesman, rebel, dust is the goal not only of chimney-sweepers but of the rich and the exalted, and a day will come, he says, when the memory of the British Empire will only be an ancient fairy-tale. These prophecies of doom, springing out of an old national jealousy and dislike, are not beyond the scope of Mr. O'Casey's talent, which can set the rivers rising and the winds howling in a formidable threat of disaster. There are words in this play, especially towards the end, that scowl and mutter ominously; and all would be perfectly in order had not Mr. O'Casey, in the course of the evening, so clearly fallen in love with the men to whose destruction they are addressed.

Harold Hobson, *Sunday Times*, 19 Aug. 1962

[O'Casey responded to these reviews in an essay entitled 'Purple Dust in Their Eyes', in *Under a Colored Cap*, p. 261-77.]

O'Casey is a damn tricky person. What appears with him to be insignificant is always of the greatest significance. Contrary to Ibsen. For O'Casey's characters, mere speaking assumes the quality of action. It is significant not merely what somebody says, but how and at what length something is being said.

Helmut Baierl, co-translator for the Berliner Ensemble production

Again and again during the overture the large artificial spider crept tirelessly out of the folds of the carefully prepared curtain and the two contrived rats made their gala appearance in front of the curtain by emerging from the holes in the prompter's box. Finally, one got to view the interior and the magic world of the old Tudor-style castle hall. Here the Irish craftsmen moved into action, emerging from holes beneath the floors as well as from the holes in the free-hanging Irish coffered ceiling. Here hens cackled and a theatrical cow went for a stroll, munching grass. Here a huge grass-roller breaks through a castle wall; there a table gets jammed within a too small doorway; until finally all dissolves into dust, into *Purple Dust*, and becomes a huge basin of water in which are cheerful Irish fish bursting with life.

Hans-Georg Simmgen,
director of the Berliner Ensemble production

[The Berliner Ensemble] performed *Purple Dust*, as it were, like a posthumous meeting between O'Casey and Brecht. Both have a lot in common: they were social realists as well as real socialists; both left behind a lifetime's work, full of intellectual energy and lyric beauty, which places them at the top of the dramatic world literature of our century. But – one should not overlook the differences, and I am only speaking now of their dramatic works: Brecht's poetic lines of argument are concentrated, brief; the pleasure is logical in the manner in which logic gives pleasure. O'Casey's plays by contrast are not less consistent, but are less concentrated; they do not delve any less deeply, but they do spread out more; they are basically rational, but romantic in many a detail and episode; sometimes they are lyrically abandoned and the final result is drawn less summarily.

Here in this production O'Casey and Brecht met – and it turned out to be a meeting worth viewing. O'Casey was divided by Brecht – and O'Casey was multiplied. Every detail, every sentence was taken to task with regard to its necessity, its function; the realism of the play was dipped in a bright, sharp, and sometimes garish light. No corner remained in the dark. The satirical contours stood out harshly and precisely. Such a performance of O'Casey, where a play is both divided as well as multiplied, would of course be only conceivable in the Berliner Ensemble; and the calculation left over no remainder: knowledge and pleasure made their twin appearance.

Gunther Cwoydrak,
The World Stage, March 1966, trans. Sigrid and Richard Weber

Purple Dust – that was wonderful! Mrs. Weigel had warned me: the production was a little crazy. But: it's bound to be. For especially within the craziness lies the comic quality of the play. The good thing is that O'Casey's message does not go by the board. . . . There are theatres, where people believe that plays with a critical social content have to be performed solemnly. But that was not Sean's intention. There is always lurking a great deal of humour, and this humour was beautifully seen here. It makes me very happy to experience the way in which O'Casey is honoured and loved here.

Eileen O'Casey in interview, *Berliner Zeitung*, May 1966

Red Roses for Me

Play in four acts.
Written: 1940–42.
First performed: Olympia Th., Dublin, 15 Mar., 1943 (dir.
Shelah Richards; with Dan O'Herlihy as Ayamonn Breydon).

Revived: People's Th., Newcastle-upon-Tyne, 25 Mar. 1943;
  Embassy Th., London, 26 Feb. 1946 (dir. Ria Mooney); Th.
  Workshop, Th. Royal, Stratford East, London, 4 May 1954
  (dir. Joan Littlewood; des. John Bury); Booth Th., New York,
  28 Dec. 1955 (dir. John O'Shaughnessy; des. Howard Bay);
  Schlosspark-Theater, Berlin, 15 Feb. 1957; Théâtre National
  Populaire, Palais de Chaillot, Paris, 9 Feb. 1961, (dir. Jean
  Vilar); Mermaid Th., London, 4 Sept. 1962 (dir. Julius
  Gellner); Deutsches Theater, Berlin, 30 Apr. 1963;
  Abbey Th., Dublin, 1967 (dir. and des. Tomas MacAnna);
  Schiller-Theater, Berlin, 19 Dec. 1977; Abbey Th., Dublin,
  10 Apr. 1980 (dir. Hugh Hunt; des. Tanya Moiseiwitsch);
  Citizens' Th., Glasgow, 14 Oct. 1982 (dir. Giles Havergal;
  des. Geoff Rose).
Published: London: Macmillan, 1942; in *Collected Plays III*; in
  Selected Plays; in *Three More Plays*; in *The Sean O'Casey
  Reader*; in *Six Plays*; and in *Complete Plays 3*. *Translated
  into*: Bulgarian, Danish, Estonian, French, German, Italian,
  Persian, Polish, Romanian, Russian, Spanish.

---

*Dublin circa 1911: Ayamonn Breydon, a poor working class
Protestant, leads a strike of railwaymen for a wage increase of a
shilling a week. Ayamonn is concerned about both the necessities
and the quality of life, and contrasting attitudes towards him
and the strike are expressed by a variety of characters with
differing political views and religious beliefs – his mother; his
girlfriend, a strict Roman Catholic and daughter of a sergeant in
the Royal Irish Constabulary; an atheist revolutionary; a
Protestant slum landlord. Ayamonn's vision of a new life for the
urban poor is shown in a lyrical passage in Act III, set by a
bridge on the banks of the Liffey, where Dublin is transformed
into a Golden City and the people dance. But on the evening of
the Easter vigil, Ayamonn is killed in a battle between the
strikers and police, sacrificed for his vision in which 'he saw the
shilling in the shape of a new world'.*

[*Red Roses for Me* is generally considered to be O'Casey's most
autobiographical play. It was premiered four months after publication.]

I was very excited and delighted when Sean O'Casey seemed pleased that I wanted to do the first production of his play *Red Roses for Me* at the Olympia Theatre. . . . I found it a difficult script to translate to the stage, but very rewarding. My outstanding memories of the production are – the set of Act III (A Bridge over the Liffey) and talking to Anne Yeats who worked with our designer, Ralph Cusack. . . . she remembers this scene on the Dublin Quays – 'Warm and colourful, rich and redolent of the Dublin of those days'. . . . My main impression now, although details are vague in my memory, is that the production . . . conveyed a tremendous sense of the colourful shabbiness of eighteenth-century Dublin. I remember the truly lovely singing by John Stephenson, who played Brennan o' the Moor, of the ballad 'Red Roses for Me'. I can still hear him. Dan O'Herlihy, now in Hollywood, gave a fine and moving performance as Ayamonn.

Shelah Richards, director of the Olympia production,
programme note to Abbey Theatre revival, 1980

James Joyce, Denis Johnston, Micheal MacLiammoir have each tried to express the soul of Dublin in art, and now . . . Sean O'Casey has made his contribution. Characteristically he chooses to express it through his picture of the rousing of the working classes from their torpor. O'Casey sees the fierce labour disputes that tore the city in the early years of the second decade of this century as the prelude to the great storms of nationalism that won us freedom. In the magnificent third act (perhaps the finest piece of expressionist writing he has ever written), he clinches his argument and weaves his story into the history of Dublin. Here his people are not alone a suffering submerged class, they are integral in a great tradition, the thousand generations of the city's past look down on them, the myriad generations of the future wait to take up the burden when it falls from their hands.

This play is a paean to Irish Labour, more especially to Dublin Labour, for it could have come only out of Dublin. Whether we agree with its sentiments or not, it is magnificent theatre, the work of a master craftsman. The play is live and vital from the rising of the curtain, and yet the plot is a mere shadowy outline of a railway strike and a protest meeting broken by a charge of mounted police. With vivid characterization and passages of dialogue in which the beauty and the power of the prose is entrancing, we are led skilfully from near realism to near symbolism, and the path is made so easy for us that we have no difficulty in keeping in accord with the mind of the author.

D.S., *Irish Independent*, 16 Mar. 1943

In this new play O'Casey has, for the first time, gained complete control of that difficult blend of realism with symbolism, prose with poetry, which he has used for his recent works. He shows with his characteristic mixture of rage and compassion, a vision of humanity striving to free itself from the squalidities in which it has somehow involved itself. And for his characters he goes to the mean streets of Dublin he knows so well.

Chief of these characters is Ayamonn Breydon, poet and idealist, who loses his life in a strike for a rise of a shilling, because 'he saw the shilling in the shape of a new world'. The actual story, however, is the least of the play's beauties. The greatest of them is the uplifting sense of being in company with a noble mind.

W.A. Darlington, Daily Telegraph, 27 Feb. 1946

Sean O'Casey has always transfigured theatre-speech, just as now – in this play's superb third act – he touches the Liffey to burnished bronze and sets an aureole around roof and pillar. Tired slum-folk shine for a moment in a splendour of aspiring youth; their feet move to the rhythms of the dance and their speech to O'Casey's dancing prose.

J.C.Trewin, The Observer, 3 Mar. 1946

It's not easy to translate the Irish gift of the gab into French. The speech of these playboys of the western world is extremely literary, or at least very rich in imagery. There is always one adjective too many. They don't say 'this table' but 'this pearly table'. . . . They don't say 'my father', but 'my good father', or 'my old rascal of a father'. If you leave that out, it is treachery. And if you leave the local colour in, you run the risk of being too 'flowery'. The Parisian audiences need to know that, in Ireland, this language is natural, its very excess is the bread and butter of conversation. An old Irish woman talked for ten minutes about my Christian name, Michel, comparing it to the local name Michael.

Michel Hobart, translator for the French production,
in Le Figaro Litteraire, 4 Feb. 1961, trans. Colin Boswell

Red Roses for Me could have been a play full of hatred and despair. Instead it is full of anger and hope. This gives . . . more force and more extension to the great appeal for justice which it contains. All the heroes reveal a tenderness, a manifest *joie de vivre*, a deep seated taste for the simplest forms of happiness which show up with even starker clarity the injustice and oppression which they run into. And in so doing, makes this injustice and oppression even more detestable. . . .

[O'Casey] had the cunning or the instinct to depict this strike from the inside, not to turn into an event of great historical moment, but to show that this strike, like other probably more violent manifestations, was one of those moments of fever, one of those reactions so necessary to the Irish people, which, coming from the deepest part of their character, with ever-increasing frequency and power, were to lead Ireland to its freedom. Thus it is in the heart of the Irish working class, dreamy, obstinate, talkative, divided, quick to fight and to pray, that the author finds his heroes.

Jacques Lemarchand, Le Figaro Litteraire,
18 Feb. 1961, trans. Colin Boswell

Of all Mr. O'Casey's plays it is perhaps the best suited to the epic style of M. Vilar. The handling of the crowd scenes here is remarkably effective, recalling in its precision and in its general impact, the Berliner Ensemble. Even the vast stage of the Palais de Chaillot seems to swarm continually with the poor of the Dublin slums. The principal characters of *Red Roses for Me* are reduced in detail, the tone of the play is lyrical rather than documentary, and M. Vilar's production methods and the training of his company have found here a perfect foil.

The Times, 25 Apr. 1961

Plays which mix realism with idealism are notoriously difficult to stage. Sean O'Casey divides the interest here between the domestic and the transcendant. There is the young poet/hero's dilemma. The girl he loves is a devout Catholic and Ayamonn is a Protestant freethinker. But, in a Dublin street on the eve of a rail strike . . . it is sheer fervent idealism that fires him with a vision of Ireland's potential greatness and, for a long transfigured moment, allows him to carry his fellow Dubliners with him into glory. . . .

Geoff Rose's set fills the stage chocablock with huge whitened packing cases and the detritus of grandeur. A whole community comes alive – quarrelsome, sentimental, histrionic, emotional, and pig-headed. Everyone remains on stage throughout, moving freely from scene to scene; playing possum till needed, and effortlessly suggesting the final off-stage violence when police and soldiery combine to break the strike in a street battle where Ayamonn loses his life as the price of his idealism.

Cordelia Oliver, The Guardian, 18 Oct. 1982

The transfiguration of Dublin in the celebrated speech of Ayamonn in Act Three . . . may be semi-mystical in sentiment and poetic in its rhythm but is neither overblown rhetoric nor empty drum beating. At the heart lies a tough-minded insistence on the need of ordinary Dubliners to possess their own city, to move beyond dreams and ruinous internecine dispute.

This marvellous production catches both the strange, haunting romanticism and the hard-edged commitment. It eschews the temptation to caricature and is never afraid of the beauty of verse or scene. At the uttering of the grand phrases which close the acts, the actors freeze into semi-classical poses, and the killing of Ayamonn, preceded by the waving of red flags, becomes a kind of apotheosis. . . .

Ireland, which aroused such conflicting emotions in O'Casey, was still 'the land that prayed too much and worked too little', yet O'Casey was impelled by a need to find, in a purely secular sense, encouragement in defeat and meaning in failure. All the schemes devised by Ayamonn, an autobiographical representation of the youthful O'Casey, end in disappointment and death. This richly-textured work, with a galaxy of splendidly sketched characters, is never pessimistic, nor is the comic spirit long absent.

Joseph Farrell, *The Scotsman*, Edinburgh, 18 Oct. 1982

Oak Leaves and Lavender

or 'A Warld on Wallpaper': play in three acts, with a Prelude.
Written: 1944.
First performed: Helsingborgs Stadsteater, Sweden, 28 Nov. 1946 (dir. K.H. Edstrom). There have been no productions of the play in either America or Ireland and only one in London: Lyric Th., Hammersmith, 13 May 1947 (dir. Walter Kerr).
Published: London: Macmillan, 1946; in *Collected Plays IV*; in *Six Plays*; and in *Complete Plays 4*. *Translated into*: French, Spanish.

In the Prelude, ghosts of eighteenth-century aristocrats dance and mourn the passing of their society and its values in the central room of Hatherleigh Manor. The scent of lavender, symbolizing death and decay, hangs in the air and remains as the action moves to the 1940s, 'during the Battle of Britain'. Dame Hatherleigh's house is now the headquarters for the local war effort. Her Irish butler, Feelim O'Morrigan, is in charge of operations, and their sons, respectively Edgar and Drishogue, are Royal Air Force Cadets. Drishogue is a communist fighting against fascism and for the people – not the British capitalists but those communists who died at Guernica. Both men are killed in an air battle. The house changes 'with the changing world outside it', and symbolically becomes a factory; a wireless broadcast reveals that the Red Army of the Soviet Union has joined the Allies; the scent of lavender returns, the ghosts reappear, and Dame Hatherleigh joins them in a strange masque-like epilogue: 'Our end makes but a beginning for others'.

(*Apr. 1940*) I have written and typed out roughly 60 pages of ideas and dialogue for a new play; and when I've done near as many more, I'll try to put it into shape. It's what you call a 'Boom Boom' play, though there are no 'Boombs' in it. I imagine, in ways, it may be an odd play. I was going to call it *Roll Out the Barrel*, but have decided to change it to *A Warald on Wallpaper*. There will be a good deal of what I think to be humour (I hope I'm right) in it; and this will be pointed with a few attempts at seriousness.

(*8 Oct. 1944*) I expect to finish my new play – *A Warald on Wallpaper* – in a fortnight or so. I hope, of course, you'll like it. I don't imagine it is in any way like most plays (like any) written around the war. It is largely a Comedy (or Farce), and is (will be) inscribed to Cuchullain, the legendary hero, who, having tied himself to a stake that he might die upright in front of his enemies, laughed long at the comic aspect of a raven slipping about in the blood that had flown from his wounds. The play opens with a prelude, shades of eighteenth-century sparks and their ladies dancing a slow minuet, and wondering in a ghostly way what is happening. They end the play, too; and between these two appearances, the major play is written. There is ne'er a bang in it anyway: I don't care a lot now for these bangs, though I had them enough in my earlier plays; and can't cavil at anyone having them in his.

O'Casey, letters to George Jean Nathan

[The sub-title is a satirical reference to Yeats's rejection of *The Silver Tassie*: 'the whole history of the world must be reduced to wallpaper in front of which the characters must pose and speak'. 'Warald' became 'World' to convey, 'world-war on wallpaper, by telescoping two words into one'.]

In performance Mr. O'Casey's new dramatic experiment in poetic prose disappoints. It attempts an impression of the Battle of Britain in terms of an eloquence which those who took part in it notably lacked; but it is not because Mr. O'Casey finds words for the inarticularly heroic that his play disappoints: rather because they are so often the wrong words and leave his theme so bare of meaning.

Land girls, members of the Home Guard, conscientious objectors, village policemen, great ladies of the county, combatant young Irishmen, and eighteenth-century ghosts dancing the minuet through the great room of this old house, all speak or chant or sing as though 'intoxicated with the exuberance of their own verbosity'. And naturally they never attain, nor does the great occasion which brings them together, the intensity and universality for which Mr. O'Casey is trying. The emotional intention is quite clear: it is never carried into effect. The young people snatch desperately at life as they comprehend it, are snatched away by life as others have made it for them, and fall aflame from the sky or are burnt on the ground; and the old people are left fixing steel hats firmly on their heads, for, as the Irish butler whose tetchy wisdom is the best of the play, says with savage resolve: 'Steel's a sensible embroidery for an ageing head to-day'. But the elegant ghosts of the old house destined to be turned into a munitions factory have the last word: 'The lavender will bloom again and the oak leaves laugh at the wind in the storm.'

The Times, 14 May 1947

One acknowledges the intention to praise Britain, even the Britain of outmoded privilege, for her stand in 1940. But as in *Within the Gates* the Irish poetic afflatus, on English lips, rings false. . . . That the heroes and heroines of the Battle of Britain – for O'Casey's purpose they are fighter pilots and their Land Girl friends – were in fact mostly gloriously mute is neither here nor there. Our stage thirsts for a drama on this subject which has the rich humour and the length of line our stage boasted in that other greatest hour, for the Armada; and with a play of this kind there is no reason whatever why grieving mothers and parting lovers should not unpack their hearts with the eloquence of a Juno. But, here, bluntly, are not the right words.

Was Mr. O'Casey too near his subject to draw it right? Is he fundamentally too Irish to be the poet of Anglo-Saxon heartbreak and pride? Apart from the two Irishmen (valid symbols of the individual Irish who joined with us), his figures are curiously hazy. Perhaps there was a natural confusion of feeling in praising England, as might be felt by an outlaw suddenly thanking the police. The stray touches of praise of the Red Army come in oddly too (where was Russia in 1940?). At all events the spell does not work.

Philip Hope-Wallace, *Time and Tide*, 24 May 1947

Cock-a-Doodle Dandy

Play in three scenes.
Written: 1947.
First performed: People's Theatre, Newcastle-upon-Tyne, 10 Dec. 1949 (dir. Peter Trower).
Revived: Carnegie Hall Playhouse, New York, 12 Nov. 1958 (dir. Philip Burton); English Stage Company, Lyceum Th., Edinburgh, 7 Sept., and Royal Court Th., London, 17 Sept. 1959 (dir. George Devine; des. Sean Kenny; with Wilfrid Lawson, J.G. Devlin, Patrick Magee, Norman Rodway, and Colin Blakely); Berliner Ensemble, 5 Jan. 1971 (dir. Werner Hecht and Hans-Georg Voigt); Théâtre de l'Est Parisien, Avignon Festival, 12 July, and Paris, 10 Oct. 1975 (dir. Guy Retoré); Lyric Th., Belfast, 5 Nov. 1975 (dir. Tomas MacAnna); Los Angeles Actors Th., California, 19 Sept. 1976 (dir. Donald Moffatt); Abbey Th., Dublin, 11 Aug. 1977 (dir. Tomas MacAnna).
Published: London: Macmillan, 1949; in *Collected Plays IV*; in *Classic Irish Drama* (Harmondsworth: Penguin, 1964); in *The Sean O'Casey Reader*; and in *Complete Plays 4*.
Translated into: Dutch, French, German, Italian, Polish, Romanian, Slovak, Spanish.

The village of Nyadnanave (gaelic for Nest of Saints), a microcosm of rural Ireland, is subject to the repressive forces of the Catholic Church, personified by the local priest, Father Domineer, and of bourgeois-capitalism, in the shape of lucrative peat-bog owner Michael Mathraun. Engaged in battle with these joyless men is the Cock, a dionysiac spirit and magician, responsible for the strange supernatural happenings that occur in and around Mathruan's house. The enchanted bird's disciples are Mathraun's daughter Loreleen, his second wife Lorna, and his maid Marion who, with the Messenger, Robin Adair (in love with Marion), become increasingly isolated from and reviled by the local population. Further events involve a strike by peat-bog workers and a dying girl's unsuccessful attempt to seek a cure at Lourdes. Father Domineer is eventually victorious in his fight against the powers of joy, love, and freedom, and, with the help of One-Eyed Larry, he exorcises the Cock from Mathraun's house; the 'cynical jester' causes havoc in retaliation but is ultimately defeated. Loreleen is prevented from escaping with Sailor Mahan, Mathraun's business partner, by a mob of vigilantes; she is dragged back to the triumphant priest who banishes her from the village. She is followed in to exile by Lorna, Marion and Robin; they 'go not towards an evil, but leave an evil behind'.

[O'Casey described *Cock-a-Doodle Dandy* as 'a secular hymn to the joy of life' and his 'favourite play'.]

Cock-a-Doodle Dandy is a play that will arouse both anger and pity in any Irishman on first impact. The anger will be *at* O'Casey – the pity will be *for* him. *Cock-a-Doodle Dandy* is a blindly and bitterly destructive blast against an Ireland that never existed outside the imagination of a lonely and homesick man in Devonshire – a fantastic mumbo-jumbo land peopled by a race of slaves who kow-tow obsequiously to a jansenistic, authoritarian, clerical tyranny that never could or would be endured in this Ireland. . . . The redeeming points . . . are that behind the distortion is an eye that sees our flaws – although it magnifies them madly; behind the savagery is a great affection for the land and its people; and behind all is a very great playwright, working at too many miles remove from the source-material he used incomparably well twenty years ago, and viewing it now through the wrong end of a telescope with a flawed and twisted lens.

Seamus Kelly, *Irish Times*, 14 Dec. 1949

This is the fantastic morality play that Mr. O'Casey wrote a decade ago in defence of joy and in condemnation of meanness, In philosophy and in the freedom of its craftsmanship, it is the grandest play of his post-war period. . . . *Cock-a-Doodle Dandy* is . . . an imaginative fantasy in which the cock crows and leaps about the landscape, evil spirits put a curse on a bottle of whisky, eerie voices terrify the joyless people and banshees explode inside the house.

There are also songs and dances, a few turns of horseplay and one or two ceremonial scenes. . . .

The last act is particularly well written, for it is decisive and merciful. Fortunately, the acting is at its best in these sombre climactic moments: Mr. Geer disconsolate before the door of his empty house, the girls on their way to some happier region, the mysterious messenger singing a farewell song.

Brooks Atkinson, *New York Times*, 13 Nov. 1958

I call the play difficult. The truth is that unless one has read it . . . one cannot feel secure in any estimate of it based on a production that is less than marvellously atune to its peculiarly mixed music. For the play is a poem and a harangue, a bitterly sad farce, a tender fantasy and a savage parody. It sings and it preaches, it guffaws and it curses. There appears to be too much outright anger in it, and while one is inclined in a certain mood to find its indignation fully justified, one cannot be altogether certain that its anger, if articulated in the proper vein, could not be turned into a beautifully wry melancholy, a heart-broken sweetness.

The play is presumably a paean to the abundant joyousness of life, but the dramatist's heart is oppressed by frustrations, his grin is distorted by outrage at the forces of bigoted religiosity which darken the landscape of his beloved country. There is no patriot more clamorously harsh than the alienated Irishman. He can express his devotion only in a lament that is rendered strident by derision and while he sheds tears of compassion, one cannot avoid the sense that they are commingled with venom.

Harold Clurman, *Nation*, New York, 29 Nov. 1958

[In choosing this play for the English Stage Company's production at the Edinburgh Festival in 1959] Devine seems to have been honouring a debt to the past. One of his first statements on joining the ESC was that he hoped to emulate the example of the Abbey Theatre, where the public 'beat each other over the head with shillelaghs'. *Cock-a-Doodle Dandy*, a bog-Irish *Bacchae* which had been waiting eleven years for a professional performance, definitely belonged in the shillelagh department, and O'Casey told Devine, 'that if I put it on in Dublin, I would be stoned'. As there was no prospect of putting that to the test (given O'Casey's ban on productions in Ireland), Devine also wanted to challenge the conventional belittlement of O'Casey as a two-play author whose talent had withered in his self-imposed exile.

Irving Wardle, *The Theatres of George Devine*
(London: Cape, 1978), p. 218-9

Objectors may say that because it sets out to tell a series of devastating home truths about Ireland, *Cock-a-Doodle Dandy* has no universal appeal and therefore no claim on the attention of playgoers outside Eire. They would be wrong. Although the satire is directed against a particular brand of priest-ridden, superstitious kill-joyism, its true target . . . is kill-joyism everywhere. O'Casey is on the side of youth against age and his symbolic figure of the Cock which seems to dreary elders to be the devil and to the young to be the harbinger of happiness is not just a local breed of fowl.

W.A. Darlington, *Daily Telegraph*, 8 Sept. 1959

Sean O'Casey has written a strange, wise, wonderful play. It is full of big ideas eloquently expressed and it has an unashamed message – the message of life. The battle between darkness and light is fought with passion and humour and verbal extravagance. The forces of religion, authority, ignorance, and superstition, represented by the priest and the two old men haggling over the price of peat, leave the hunt to exorcise the demon cock chosen by O'Casey as a symbol of the unchecked human spirit.

Like Blake, O'Casey sees ordinary people struggling against the 'mind-forged manacles of man', and in this play he expresses his deepest feelings about the dilemma not only of Ireland but of a world where the human spirit is crushed, where knowledge is feared and love denied. . . . George Devine's production is colourful and imaginative and he is not afraid of emphasizing O'Casey's symbolism with all the tricks of stagecraft. The two old men are splendidly played by J.G. Devlin and Wilfrid Lawson.

H.A., *Daily Worker*, 10 Sept. 1959

[Invited to see Devine's production at the Royal Court Theatre in London, O'Casey] welcomed the invitation to see his favourite work. It was a good many years since he had been in any London theatre; with his bad eyesight he had to sit fairly close to the stage, but in spite of it, and though he could not hear half of Lawson's dialogue, he acknowledged the general quality of the acting, and, curiously, was not in the least critical: happy, I think, that ten years after it had been published, the play had achieved this major production. I had a job to get him to attend George Devine's party on the stage after the performance, but he gave way and met there John Osborne with whom he was photographed, Sean as the Angry Old Man and Osborne as the Angry Young Man, tags invented by the theatre's press representative, George Fearon.

Eileen O'Casey, *Sean* (London: Macmillan, 1972), p. 273

There is no doubting who's the star of the latest new Abbey production of Sean O'Casey's *Cock-a-Doodle Dandy* – it is, of course, a noble red-feathered cock, a demon bird . . . who symbolizes a joyful spirit of life in the Irish scene. It is the most total performance I've seen at the Abbey for years, for here words, sound and lighting all merge beautifully to set the seal on a glorious romp. . . .

In a lovely striking set by Brian Collins, director Tomas MacAnna, obviously in sympathy with the play, pulls out all the stops to set the stage alight with song and dance and some very witty O'Casey lines. As the Cock terrorizes and bewitches the citizens of Nyadnanave . . . O'Casey finds time to have a few old fashioned swipes at the Church and the knights of Colambanus. . . .

He sometimes gets very close to the spirit of Ireland (that Ireland of the 'thirties and 'forties, certainly not the 'seventies) as the cock dances and crows, rousing up commotion among the young anxious for uninhibited life, and the indignation and hatred among those who demand self denial. *Cock-a-Doodle Dandy* is by no means a great play: sometimes it is over verbose and O'Casey takes much too long to tell his one huge joke. But one must admire the style, the sparkle, the sheer gaiety of the piece.

Gus Smith, *Sunday Independent*, Dublin, 14 Aug. 1977

Hall of Healing

'A Sincerious Farce in One Scene'.
Written: 1949.
First performed: Three Plays Company, Yugoslav-American
  Hall, New York, 1 May 1952 (dir. Joseph Papirofsky).
Revived: Unity Th., London, 22 May, 1953 (dir. David
  Dawson); Kammerspiele des Deutschen Theaters, Berlin,
  6 Oct. 1965 (dir. Adolf Dresen); Abbey Th., Dublin, 28 Feb.
  1966 (dir. Tomas MacAnna); Théâtre National de Strasbourg,
  March 1978 (dir. Jean-Pierre Vincent).
Published: in *Collected Plays III*; in *Five One-Act Plays*; and in
  Complete Plays 3. *Translated into*: French, German,
  Russian, Turkish.

A winter's day in the waiting room of the Dublin Parish Dispensary for the Poor, 'where the ragged, the cold, and the sick poor gathered, hustled in and hustled out again, as if they had no claim on life, and it was an impudent thing for them to be seeking the comfort of health'. The general condition of the people is highlighted by the particular situation of Red Muffler, his wife, and their consumptive daughter whose death is the consequence of the indifference of the authorities and the patients' acceptance of a pernicious system.

[Writing to his friend Jack Daly on 11 July 1949, O'Casey informed him: 'Have written a One-act play to keep my hand in – experience of mine in a Dublin Poor Dispensary, the time you and I and Will Kelly were alive on the Dublin Streets . . .'. The play was first staged as part of a triple bill (with *Bedtime Story* and *Time to Go*) by an off-Broadway group whose acting was 'frantically inadequate' with no 'sense of genre style for Irish drama'. When Unity Theatre staged the London premiere, Donald Douglas in the *Daily Worker* described the play as 'a passionate attack with all O'Casey's guns blazing.' He added: 'His twin targets are the arrogance of authority when it is imposed upon, and not derived, from the people; and the cowardice of the people when they fail to combine against the power that humiliates and destroys them' (29 May 1953). The play formed part of a 'splendid double bill' (with Lorca's *Yerma*) at the Abbey in 1966.]

Hall of Healing is brimful of comedy expressed in gloriously flamboyant O'Casey language. This most engaging little play has never been seen in Dublin before, though why it has not been paired with *Shadow of a Gunman* is a mystery. It is bitterly tragic in its impact, which is all the stronger because of the sparkling comedy, and under Tomas MacAnna's direction the Abbey company play it superbly.

Desmond Rushe, *Irish Independent*, 2 Mar. 1966

Emphasis [in the Strasbourg production] is laid on colours, light and warmth in this 'Hall' where people come for wonders and mirages – short-lived though they may be – and for the warmth of others as opposed to outer darkness.

The director has purposefully dismissed any hint that the place might be a cold, grim, grey harbinger of death. . . . At the same time there is in all this a definite imitation of a church atmosphere, all the more so as an organ is heard playing throughout the play – in a neighbouring church, as the stage directions go.

The room ... has no wall at the back and the space for acting extends from the floodlit foreground straight out into the darkness. Now and again high winds sweeping from the right blow in a snowstorm, or some characters enter with their caps soaked with water. The latter are all ghost-like, all dressed in nondescript clothes with only a bright-coloured muffler or a bright-coloured pair of socks as an identification tag: the filthy uniform of the underdog. ...

A remarkable achievement altogether, in conveying through this production the peculiarity of O'Casey's world. ... The expressionistic scenery symbolizing light and darkness is skilfully combined here with the realistic rendering of the warmth of the hall and the bad weather outside thanks to technical tricks displayed for all to see; the characters are not content with symbolizing psychological or social attitudes (revolt, despair, acceptance) but at the same time they are shown living realistically as they wait and queue up through the plainness of everyday life dialogues – the type of language to be heard in the waiting-rooms.

Now, the director's actual stroke of genius is the way unexpected glimpses of charmingly peaceful landscapes appear in flashes on the blackness of the blackcloth – utter despair giving way to visions so to speak. Luminous flashes, hardly perceptible at first owing to their brevity, then growing more and more perceptible, reveal a landscape with fir-trees in the moonlight or the sun setting on a lake. They suddenly break and transfigure the desperate emptiness of outer darkness against which the play is performed. ... By means of this unexpected, intermittent transfiguration, Jean-Pierre Vincent has rediscovered spontaneously the revolutionary role of dreams that the dramatist himself once emphasized in his famous scene of *Red Roses for Me*.

Emile Jean Dumay, *Sean O'Casey Review*, V, 1 (Fall 1978)

Time to Go

'A Morality Comedy in One Act'.
Written: 1949.
First performed: Three Plays Company, Yugoslav-American
    Hall, New York, 7 May 1952 (dir. Albert Kipton),
Revived: Unity Th., London, 22 May 1953 (dir. Ivor Pinkus);
    Th. de Lys, New York, 22 Mar. 1960.
Published: in *Collected Plays IV*; in *Five One-Act Plays*; and in
    Complete Plays 4. *Translated into*: French, German, Russian.

It is in O'Casey's most difficult strain: full of whimsy and fantasy. But the core is hard and glittering and the moral is inescapable. The set is an Irish country town with the inn of Flagonson and the store of Farrell prominent. Both men are money-makers. Their friends are money-makers. They differ among themselves on non-essentials – Farrell, for instance, attacks the Church in public while he subscribes to its funds in private – but in essentials they stick together like one man. And that essential is: they must capture and silence the people to whom money means nothing and less than nothing: the people who will ask too little for the goods they have to sell and who refuse to pay too much for the goods they buy. The man and woman who represent this uncommercial ideal are, indeed, captured and taken away in handcuffs. But the end is joyous, for the heretics escape. And across the persistent noise of jingling gold comes the free call of the men and women who can never be silenced; the men and women to whom honour and truth and the joy of life are the real standards.

Donal Douglas, *Daily Worker*, 29 May 1953

Bedtime Story

'An Anatole Burlesque in One Act'.

Written: 1950.

First performed: Three Plays Company, Yugoslav-American Hall, New York, 7 May 1952 (dir. Joseph Papipofsky).

Revived: Th. Guild, Playhouse Th., New York, 15 Apr. 1959 (dir. Hume Cronyn); Theater im 3 Stock der Volksbühne, Berlin, 20 Sept, 1959 (dir. Hagen Müller-Stahl); Théâtre de Bourgogne, France, 1962 (dir. A. Steiger); Carouge Th., Geneva, Jan. 1967; Abbey Th. Company, Peacock Th., Dublin, 27 June 1972 (dir. John Lynch); Bristol Old Vic, 28 Aug. 1985 (dir. Paul Unwin).

Published: in *Collected Plays IV*; in *Selected Plays*; in *Five One-Act Plays*; in *The Sean O'Casey Reader*; and in *Complete Plays 4*. *Translated into*: Estonian, French, German, Hungarian, Persian, Polish, Russian, Spanish.

John Jo Mulligan, a respectable Catholic bachelor, invites Angela Nightingale, 'a gay lass', back to his room in Miss Mossie's boarding house. Terrified that his landlady and fellow lodger, Daniel Halibut, should discover her, and more than a little remorseful about his indiscretion, Mulligan tries to get Angela quietly out of the house in the middle of the night. After putting up a spirited resistance Angela eventually leaves, but not before she has relieved him of money and goods. Mossie and Halibut mistake Mulligan's consequent fury for madness and call a policeman, a doctor, and a nurse to deal with him.

[O'Casey described *Bedtime Story* as 'out of my usual manner, a comedy, fanciful in a way, too.' The sub-title is a reference to the one-act plays about a philanderer by Arthur Schnitzler collectively called *Anatol*.]

There is more than a low-comedy romp in *Bedtime Story*. Beneath the surface fun, it satirizes the timidity and respectability of the perfect hypocrite. It expresses the O'Casey contempt for the pious charlatan. By playing it all in one key and one tempo, Miss Tandy and Mr. Cronyn miss the most genuine part of the comedy, which is the satire of character in the midst of a tense situation.

Brooks Atkinson, *New York Times*, 16 Apr. 1959

The Bishop's Bonfire

'A Sad Play within the Tune of a Polka' in three acts.
Written: 1954.
First performed: Gaiety Th., Dublin, 28 Feb. 1955 (dir. Tyrone Guthrie; with Cyril Cusack as Codger Sleehaun).
Revived: Theater im Ballhop, Hannover, June 1956 (dir. Heinz Dietrich Kenter); Mermaid Th., London, 26 July 1961 (dir. Frank Dunlop); Schlosspark-Theater, Berlin, 16 Dec. 1972 (dir. Wilfried Minks); Kammerspiele, Munich, Dec. 1982 (dir. Thomas Langhoff).
Published: London: Macmillan, 1955; in *Six Plays*; and in *Complete Plays 5*. *Translated into*: French, German, Italian, Russian.

An assortment of quarrelsome workmen are decorating the house of Ballyoonagh's wealthiest citizen, Councillor Reiligan, in preparation for the visit of a Roman Catholic Bishop. Reiligan has a son, Michael, an army lieutenant, and two daughters: Keelin, in love with Daniel, a labourer, and Foorawn, in love with Manus, who has renounced the priesthood for her. They are encouraged in their relationships by the young curate, Father Boheroe, but opposed by Reiligan and his ally Cannon Burren. Keelin is forced to give up Daniel in favour of an arranged match with a wealthy old farmer (the Bishop's brother); Forawn takes a vow of chastity, discovers the disillusioned Manus stealing church money, and in the ensuing quarrel he shoots her. As she dies she writes a suicide note absolving him of guilt. As part of the festivities to mark the Bishop's visit a huge bonfire of 'bad' books and 'evil' pictures is to be lit. In the face of the repressive alliance of Church and State the Codger, an aged but 'jaunty and defiant' odd-job-man, and Father Boheroe stand for joy and freedom. But the Codger is banished for his outspoken criticism of Reiligan; Father Boheroe who believes that 'merriment may be a way of worship' is defeated and leaves the village; and the bonfire is lit.

[Described by O'Casey as 'an outspoken play, with a good deal of humour, and some sad moments', he suspected that it might cause 'a storm' if it were to be produced in Dublin. He was to be proved right when, in Feb. 1955, ten days before the play was due to open at the Gaiety Theatre, an attack against the playwright was mounted in the *Standard*, a Catholic weekly newspaper printed in Dublin. Excerpts from O'Casey's autobiographies appeared on the front page of one issue with the intention of demonstrating his anti-Catholic attitudes, and the following week (25 Feb.) a further article declared: 'It is one of the contradictions of modern life that he should be offered a stage in the capital city of the country most steadfastly ranged against the enemies who are his friends. . . . Where is the native self-respect?' Consequently the opening night was sold out and, as expected, the event, witnessed by 'the most distinguished audience assembled in a Dublin theatre for many years', did not pass without incident.]

Dublin, Feb 28 – The final curtain went down tonight on the premiere of Sean O'Casey's new play . . . amid rounds of applause from most of the audience and boos and hisses from a group of young men in the gallery. For an hour before the play began the groups of young men . . . lined the approaches to the theatre and demonstrated. They were still there in force near midnight when the crowds were emerging at the close.

The audience laughed heartily at the comedy of the piece. Then in the final act when Paul Farrell, who played the part of a parish priest, used the words 'I am ashamed of you' to other characters in the play a chorus of voices from the gallery called out 'We are ashamed of you'. For the last few minutes of the play there were constant interruptions and catcalls. After the final curtain Cyril Cusack stepped forward and addressed the objectors, first speaking in Irish. He was hissed when he said 'I am proud to have brought back Sean O'Casey to Dublin'.

New York Times, 1 Mar. 1955

Sean O'Casey exploded a stick of dramatic dynamite on the stage of the Gaiety Theatre tonight with the world premiere of his feverishly awaited play *The Bishop's Bonfire*. . . . This rebel son of a Dublin back street sought a provocative peace with his fellow countrymen by making what is, even for him, an extraordinarily bitter mockery of the priesthood. . . . From the frenzy of festive preparation, the pride, follies, fears, and pious superstitions of the local big-wigs and riff-raff O'Casey draws a compassion for the weakness of the common man which is as deep as his contempt for the power of the Church. Indeed, he makes such an unctious villain of the priest and mixes the profane so savagely with the sacred in this cauldron of swearing, praying, drinking, bullying, and grovelling, that the play positively cries out for trouble. . . .

It is not so much a play as a strange mosaic of many plays, a confusion of tragedies and comedies which surveys the bishop's home town through a haze of alcohol, a blaze of religious fervour, and a murk of disillusion. . . . It is an ugly play beautifully told. It may provoke anger, but the sheer poetry of it, recalling the old O'Casey magic more often than we cared to expect, can provoke only admiration.

Cecil Wilson, *Daily Mail*, 1 Mar. 1955

In fairness to himself as a creative writer, Sean O'Casey should return to Ireland without delay. At present he is completely out of touch with modern Irish life and thought. . . . O'Casey's picture of the Ireland of today . . . is about as truthful as if a Russian royalist were to try to write a drama about Soviet Moscow, basing his knowledge on material in *Pravda*. . . . Tyrone Guthrie's direction was disappointingly slow and there were many loose ends. Now and then in the first two acts Guthrie seemed to be aiming at a Chekov-like atmosphere; these moments were the most successful. The best acting came from Cyril Cusack as the codger, a sort of Christy Mahon at the latter end of his life.

J.J.F., *Evening Herald*, Dublin, 1 Mar. 1955

The Irish never forgive those they have insulted. Back from long exile came Sean to Dublin, and his compatriots hissed his play at curtain-fall. At the first night of Mr. O'Casey's *The Bishop's Bonfire* there were more stage Irishmen in the house than in the cast, and by the first interval venomous tongues were already lamenting the play's failure. Those who had uprooted the author now charged him with being too parochial. How, they jeered, could a man from an urban working-class Protestant family write well about a rural middle-class Catholic family? Some blamed the director, picturing Tyrone Guthrie as an ambulance which had run over the man it was summoned to help. Others excoriated the cast. In the congress of feud and polemic the play was forgotten.

And what are the faults? That Mr. O'Casey's genius, once tragi-comic, had declined into a state best described as manic-depressive; that his hand had lost its sureness in shifting from mood to mood; and there were two plays, one ghastly, one gorgeous, in unhappy juxtaposition. The depressive (or serious) theme is youth's subser-vience to authority. . . .

What matters is the manic half of the play. Here, dealing with the wild inconsequent rustics . . . Mr. O'Casey hits his full stride as the old mocker and fantastic ironist, ever happier with tongue in cheek than hand on heart. Broad comedy of protest was always the best Irish vein, and Mr. O'Casey strikes it rich. . . . The elation of these quarrelsome, gin-swigging scenes is tremendous; you feel Mr. O'Casey had to get the characters drunk to account for the boldness of their utterance. . . .

And why are these hirelings so free of speech? Because, as one of them says: 'Me soul's me own particular compendium. Me soul's me own spiritual property, complete an' entire, verbatim in all its concernment.' They abound in their own sense, and while they are about, shouting loud or muttering 'sotto vossie', the play magnifies life as gloriously as it magnifies language. Mr. O'Casey was never a great thinker; he is no longer a great craftsman; but he remains a great singer.

Kenneth Tynan, *The Observer*, 6 Mar. 1955,
reprinted in *Curtains*, p. 83-5

What upsets many people about this play is its blending of farce, tragedy, and poetry. Though they have been brought up in this traditional English blend since they read their first Shakespeare play, for some reason they are reluctant to accept it here. I cannot think why, for the different styles are beautifully and effortlessly bound together. Perhaps the explanation lies in the fact that the intellectual, or sophisticated playgoers who share O'Casey's views nonetheless wrinkle their noses at elements of farce and melodrama which they regard as only fit for the Whitehall and Players respectively. The point is that O'Casey is appealing to a wide, popular audience without the commercial vacuity of wide, popular entertainment.

Peter Roberts, *Plays and Players*, Sept. 1961

Although German playgoers generally admire O'Casey – particularly his *Juno and the Paycock* and *The Plough and the Stars* – they are usually disappointed at the direction he receives here. There is an undercurrent of bitterness and grief that the German directors seem somehow to miss in their over-simplified productions. Thomas Langhoff, however, seems to have got it right this time with his *The Bishop's Bonfire* where realism is mixed with surrealism, where singing and dancing seems to be the result of underlying desperation, where laughter is fused with weeping.

Langhoff has presented O'Casey's characters as pure theatre figures – as clowns of desperation. And the setting by Jurgen Rose emphasizes Langhoff's ambivalent style for his setting is of 'theatrical' rooms – the walls are in oblique perspective so that instead of an expected rear wall you perceive a street, trees, and a drunkard. For once, though the production lasts the now mandatory four hours, it is never boring.

Michael Skasa, *Plays and Players*, Jan. 1983

The Drums of Father Ned

'A Mickrocosm of Ireland' in three acts, with a 'Prerumble'.
Written: 1957.
First performed: Little Th., Lafayette, Indiana, 25 Apr. 1959, (dir. Jeanne Orr and Robert Hogan).
  Revived: Queen's Th., Hornchurch, 8 Nov. 1960 (dir. David Phethean); Le Cothurne, Lyon, 1963 (dir. M.N. Marechal); Olympia Th., Dublin, 6 June 1966 (dir. and des. Tomas

MacAnna); Lyric Th., Belfast, 1 Apr. 1980 (dir. Joseph Long); Abbey Th., Dublin, 9 May 1985 (dir. Tomas MacAnna).
Published: London: Macmillan, 1960; in *The Sean O'Casey Reader*; and in *Complete Plays 5. Translated into*: Czech, French, German, Italian, Russian.

Prerumble: the early 1920s in the town of Doonavale. Binnington and McGilligan, once friends, now enemies – a Free Stater and Republican respectively – are provoked by the Black and Tans, but they hate each other more than the British. A mysterious Echo repeats and mocks their words. Present: Binnington, now the Mayor, and McGilligan, Deputy Mayor – still refusing to speak to each other but willing to do business deals – object to the joyous spirit in which the young people are preparing for the Tostal. Binnington's son, Michael, and McGilligan's daughter, Nora, despite parental opposition, are lovers and disciples of Father Ned, symbol of love and the joy of life. The priest never appears, but can be heard beating his drum as he rehearses for the Tostal procession. Whenever the town elders or the repressive priest, Father Fillifogue, criticize the behaviour or attitudes of the young people, their words are mocked by the Echo or obliterated by the drumming. Father Ned's influence inspires the young to realize their plans for the Tostal, and Michael and Nora decide to run for the offices of Mayor and Deputy Mayor, effectively ridding the town of the old order.

[In 1957 the play was to have been performed in the Theatre Festival which formed part of the Tostal held annually in Dublin. Productions of Alan McClelland's dramatization of James Joyce's *Ulysses*, entitled *Bloomsday*, and three mime plays by Samuel Beckett were also planned. The Catholic Archbishop of Dublin, John Charles McQuaid, refused to celebrate a votive mass to open the Tostal if *The Drums of Father Ned* and *Bloomsday* were included in the programme. After much debate the two plays were dropped and Beckett withdrew his three. As a result of this controversy O'Casey banned all professional productions of his plays in Dublin during his lifetime. The ban was only lifted when the Abbey was invited to participate in the World Theatre Season at the Aldwych Theatre, London, in 1964. The play received its premiere at the Lafayette Little Theatre, Indiana, USA in 1959.]

Father Ned is a cross between the cock in *Cock-a-Doodle Dandy* and one or two good priests O'Casey has heard of but never met. We see him through the young people who are all acting under his inhibition-releasing influence. As one of the boys says, 'We must fight what is old and stale and vicious, the hate, the meanness, their policies preach, and make way for the young and the thrusting.' By the play's end the young people are winning by a landslide, and even the old are becoming less scared of 'the music of life'. . . .

O'Casey himself has called this an idle laughing play, so the production here has taken him at his word and emphasized the fun. There are some excellent vigorous performances that bring out the satire for audiences that find O'Casey's unconventional form and colloquial remarks about Ireland a bit bewildering. While the company falls short of doing full justice to O'Casey's forceful lyricism, it has surpassed what one would expect from a community theatre performance of a kind of material that Broadway has yet to do satisfactorily.

Henry Hewes, *Saturday Review of Literature*, 9 May 1959

It's not a great play. It's not even a good play. But as set and produced by Tomas MacAnna . . . it is a first-class piece of theatre which shows that the O'Casey apprenticeship at the old Queen's paid off in its own way, and that he learned nothing much from his later tutorship at the feet of Augusta Gregory, Yeats, and Robinson. . . .

It's great stuff, full of the criticism that the new Ireland deserves, but equally full of the innocent non-knowledge of the new Ireland that O'Casey worked for through his press clippings. It's a good epitaph for its author, inasmuch as it's a good plea for rebellious youth, written by a good rebel.

Seamus Kelly, *Irish Times*, 7 June 1966

Behind the Green Curtains

Play in three scenes.
Written: 1959.
First performed: University of Rochester, New York State,
   5 Dec. 1962 (dir. and des. Robert Hogan).
Revived: Theater der Stadt, Cottbus, German Democratic
   Republic, 20 Nov. 1965 (dir. Friedrich Siebert and Rolf
   Winkelgrund); Project Arts Centre, Dublin, 22 July 1975 (dir.
   Frank Murphy).

Published: London: Macmillan, 1961; and in *Complete Plays* 5.
Translated into: French, German.

On the one hand, it seems a straightforward satire of the social and religious conscience of Dublin in the 'fifties: a young industrialist, Senator Chatastray, a patron of the arts, is put to the test of his liberal convictions by two allied events. An Irish writer, Lionel Robartes – uneasy shades of Yeats – has died and Chatastray must face the ire of the Catholic establishment if he enters the Protestant church for his funeral. In the third act he is under pressure – together with his coterie of 'artists' – to march in a Catholic anti-Communist procession. In both tests he fails.

It is a theme with certain, if rather hackneyed, possibilities. Had O'Casey handled it in a totally realistic idiom he would have had to give his characters more depth of psychological truth, more subtlety of motive and action. Instead, almost every character, the routine Marxist idealist, the brutal Catholic fascist, the craven ensemble of pseudo-intellectuals, become crude mouthpieces for their different ideologies. The action becomes schematic, perfunctory, and unconvincing. If he had followed another method, also present in the stage directions, he might have produced a purely symbolic play in which the debate might have been an interesting ballet of ideas. In short the text does not intrinsically define its style of production.

Augustine Martin, *Sean O'Casey Review*, II, 1 (Fall 1975)

The Moon Shines on Kylenamoe

Sketch in one act.
Written: 1959.
First performed: ANTA Company, Th. de Lys, New York,
     30 Oct. 1962 (dir. John O'Shaughnessy).
Revived: Kammerspiele des Deutschen Theaters, 6 Oct. 1965
     (dir. Adolf Dresen); Abbey Th. Company, Peacock Th.,
     Dublin, 14 Aug. 1976 (dir. Tomas MacAnna).
Published: in *Behind the Green Curtains and Other Plays*
     (London: Macmillan, 1961); and in *Complete Plays* 5.
Translated into: Danish, German, Persian.

Lord Leslieson of Ottery St. Oswald alights at Kylenamoe station in search of the British Prime Minister (on holiday in the area) to whom he must deliver important dispatches. Kylenamoe is a desolate spot, devoid of modern amenities and young people, but despite a series of confrontations and confusions the Lord eventually gets on his way in a donkey cart.

Figuro in the Night

Play in two scenes.
Written: 1959.
First performed: Hofstra University Playhouse, New York, 4
    May 1962 (dir. Mirim Tulin),
Revived: ANTA Company, Th. de Lys, New York, 30 Oct. 1962
    (dir. John O'Shaughnessy); Abbey Th. Company, Peacock
    Th., Dublin, 14 Aug. 1975.
Published: in *Behind the Green Curtains and Other Plays*
    (London: Macmillan, 1961); and in *Complete Plays 5*.
Translated into: German.

A statue of 'a Young Lad ... doing an Obscene and Most Indecent Action under the Guise of an Innocent Fountain' appears in Dublin's main street to the delight of the young and liberal-minded, and the consternation of the old and puritanical. A Birdlike Lad (suggesting a crow) announces: 'Figuro is an abounding joy everywhere at last'. The young people take up this theme and, ignoring the disapproval of their elders, join in a celebratory dance.

Mr. O'Casey says that *Figuro in the Night* is 'prayerfully and solemnly dedicated to what is known as "The Ferocious Chastity of Ireland".' In a ruefully affectionate way he breaks into a sunny, twinkling Irish smile that does not quite hide his irony and considers what might happen when a statue of a vigorous youth suddenly appears in the center of Dublin. Since the statue has provocative proportions, it naturally fascinates the young girls who have been trained to restrain their emotions. The playwright, however, particularly scrutinizes their disappointed grumbling, mumbling elders who have regrettably led unfulfilled, loveless lives. . . .

Paul Gardner, *New York Times*, 31 Oct. 1962

a: Autobiographies

O'Casey published six volumes of autobiography
between 1939 and 1954, detailed separately below.
These were also published collectively in two
volumes as *Mirror in My House* (New York:
Macmillan, 1956), and as *Autobiographies 1* and *2*
(London: Macmillan, 1963, repr. 1981; and London:
Pan Books, 1980).

As for my own 'Auto-biography', it was not first-conceived
as such, but just as incidents I had experienced. Indeed,
three of them appeared in print before the idea of a
biography came into my head. 'Royal Residence', 'Battle
Royal' – these in the *Yale Quarterly* and in *Virginia
Quarterly* attached to Charlottesville University; and a
third, 'A Protestant Kid Thinks of the Reformation', in *The
American Spectator*, then edited by George Jean Nathan.
So the idea came to me and grew expansively out and down
deep, so that a letter I have before me, from Macmillan's
dated July 1938, tells me the material sent in was 60,000
words. They thought that amount would make a book, but
would prefer 75,000 words. I evidently sent word saying
material was plentiful (the ideas were growing), and that I
would send in additional chapters. ... I first intended to
take titles for the work from 'First the Green Blade, then the
Corn, then the Full Corn in my Ear', but the rapid
development of what I was conceiving in my mind,
additional ideas crowding in after the conception of
previous ideas, made me alter the titles to the present ones
which top the various volumes.

O'Casey, letter to William J. Maroldo, 10 Aug. 1962

I Knock at the Door: 'Swift glances back at things that
made me, / Knock, and it shall be opened unto you.'
London: Macmillan, 1939. [Written during the
1930s, and covering the years 1880-92.]
Pictures in the Hallway: 'Time flies over us, but leaves
its shadow behind'. New York: Macmillan, 1942.
[Written 1939-41, and covering the years
1892-1905.] Adaptation for a staged reading by Paul

Shyre presented at the YM-YWH Poetry Center, New York, 27 May 1956, and published by Samuel French, 1957; recorded 14 and 29 Mar. 1957, and issued by Riverside Records. Adaptation for a staged reading by Patrick Fuge and David Krause presented at the Lantern Theatre, Dublin, 4 Aug. 1965.

Drums under the Windows: 'Study that house. I think about its jokes and stories'. London: Macmillan, 1945. [Written 1942-44, and covering the years 1905-16.] Adaptation for a staged reading by Paul Shyre, presented at the Cherry Lane Theatre, New York, 13 Oct. 1960; published by Dramatists Play Service, 1962. Adaptation for a staged reading by Patrick Funge and David Krause presented at the Lantern Theatre, Dublin, 21 July 1970.

Inishfallen, Fare Thee Well: 'The wheel of th' wagon's broken,/ It ain't goin' to turn no more;/The wheel of th' wagon's broken,/An' there's weeds round th' ranch-house door'. London: Macmillan, 1949. [Written 1945-47, and covering the years 1917-26.] Adaptation for the stage by Patrick Funge and David Krause presented at the Lantern Theatre, Dublin, 24 July 1972.

Rose and Crown: 'This is the porcelain clay of human kind'. London: Macmillan, 1952. [Written 1947-51 and covering the years 1926-35.]

Sunset and Evening Star: 'You cannot prevent the birds of sadness from flying over your head, but you can prevent them from building nests in your hair (Chinese proverb), I'm gonna wash 'em all outa my hair'. London: Macmillan, 1954. [Written 1951-53, and covering the years 1936-53.]

In a letter dated 7 May 1951, O'Casey wrote to George Jean Nathan that he had just sent the manuscript of *Rose and Crown* to Macmillan, and was 'jotting down notes for, I hope, the last one – *Goodbye at the Door.*' The title was presumably meant to echo the first volume, and round off the series. The title was changed to *Sunset and Evening Star* (the opening line of Tennyson's valedictory poem 'Crossing the Bar'), but the reference to the first book was made visually in the design of the dust-jacket (as with all the others, designed by O'Casey): on the first one a large Celtic Cross dominates, in front of which a young boy knocks on a door; on the last one the same cross provides the background to an old man drinking a toast in front of a half open door.

b: Correspondence

The Letters of Sean O'Casey, Volume I: 1910-1941, ed. David
   Krause. New York: Macmillan; London: Cassell, 1975.
   [Contains 653 letters by O'Casey; 124 letters to or about
   O'Casey; 21 news reports and reviews by or about O'Casey.]
The Letters of Sean O'Casey, Volume II: 1942-54, ed. David
   Krause. New York: Macmillan, 1980. [Contains 807 letters
   by O'Casey; 15 letters by others to or about O'Casey; 5
   reviews of O'Casey's work; an article and a statement to the
   press by O'Casey. Volume III (forthcoming) will cover the
   years 1955-1964.]

c: Miscellaneous Poetry and Prose

Windfalls. London: Macmillan, 1934. [Collection of stories,
   poems, and plays, written 1916-34.]
The Flying Wasp. London: Macmillan, 1937. [Collection of
   essays in which O'Casey gives his views on critics and the
   theatre.]
The Green Crow. New York: George Braziller, 1956. [Consists
   of three sections: articles reprinted from *The Flying Wasp*;
   articles 'On Diverse Subjects', reprinted from various journals,
   and four short stories from *Windfalls*.]
Feathers from the Green Crow. ed. Robert Hogan. Columbia:
   University of Missouri Press, 1962. [Selection of O'Casey's
   early writings, including articles on political and social
   subjects, songs, a lament for Thomas Ashe, a history of the
   Irish Citizen Army, four short stories, and two one-act plays
   (*Kathleen Listens In* and *Nannie's Night Out*).]
Under a Colored Cap. London: Macmillan, 1963. [Collection of
   twelve pieces, all except one written within the last ten years
   of his life, of which nine are published for the first time.]
Blasts and Benedictions. London: Macmillan, 1967. [Essays and
   stories written between 1926 and 1964, selected and
   introduced by Ronald Ayling.]
The Sean O'Casey Reader, ed. with an introduction by Brooks
   Atkinson. New York: St. Martin's Press, 1968. [The contents
   of this anthology have all been previously published in book
   form, but it also includes a bibliography of secondary source
   material to 1964 by Charles A. Carpenter.]

I was interested in St John Ervine's article in *The Observer* on the use of the aside in modern drama. Playwrights and managers are afraid of so many things and think too much of their audiences. They are afraid of soliloquy and pause in drama, and I believe that audiences are not as stupid as the dramatists imagine. I am irritated by being told of things I must not do in plays. . . .

England is waiting for the greatest English dramatist who will write about his own people. The playwrights of today turn out tiny plays about little society ladies and gentlemen with scraps of photographic dialogue. They throw life out of focus. Hardly any of them attempt to portray the life of today with imagination and passion. Recently I read in an article which offered advice to young playwrights that Mr. Noel Coward and Mr. Frederick Lonsdale should be studied. Shakespeare, the Elizabethans, the Restoration dramatists, and Shaw are the men to study.

I would make it a penal offence . . . for any man to write a play without being able to declaim two or three of Shakespeare's plays by heart. Shakespeare was my education. When I was a boy in Dublin thirty years ago, the Benson Company came to the city, and I spent all my small wages and went without food in order to see all the plays that were performed. I could hardly read or write at the time. . . . I learned to read by Shakespeare and used to act the plays in my room . . . and when I was seventeen, I wrote a comedy called *Withered Heather*. Some time after that I belonged to the drama group in the National Club. The members were content to imitate the Abbey Players, perform the same plays, in order to become little Arthur Sinclair's. I suggested that it would be a good idea to play something that had never been acted before, and I wrote *Frost in the Flower*, a two-act comedy based on a family in the club. It was so near to the characters that it was never performed, but the play was sent to the Abbey and the directors sent me a detailed criticism. That was really my start. . . .

From an interview with George Walter Bishop,
The Observer, 6 Oct. 1929,
reprinted in *The Sting and the Twinkle*

When *Within the Gates* was first performed in London, some of the English critics began to run around in circles, rumble out protests, and do everything but face firmly the form of drama that had been impudently thrust upon them. It was over their heads, and they immediately began to try to trample it under their feet. They were perplexed, and then they were frightened. Like the Bishop in the play, they called for a fuller manifestation of life, but when it came, they fled from before it and hurried for refuge in the ranks of the down-and-out critics. One highballed critic complained that the play was not 'a study of the whole seething brew of life'. He murmured resentment against a bitter comment on a land 'trying to live according to its ancient lights'. They are, indeed, ancient lights in more ways than one. Another said, 'the character who arises out of the ruck is called 'The Dreamer', and that's a pity, for if one thing is more certain than another in these troubled times it is that the day for dreaming is behind us – far, far behind us'. This fool failed to see that The Dreamer is always the first to rise out of the ruck of things. . . .

The first Dreamer is the Holy Ghost. But this fool had forgotten all about that. These English critics have become old and doddering minds in the theatre acclaiming an ageing and withering form, and the marching drama is leaving them behind with their dead hope and their dead faith. They have pilloried drama too long to the form of dead naturalism, and all fresh and imaginatively minded dramatists are out to release drama from the pillory of naturalism and send her dancing through the streets.

We have become too clever by half. Our graceful and polished manner of playwriting has sucked the life and soul out of the drama. For a long time the drama was the most popular and most powerful of the arts. It was majestic in the days of the Greeks and magnificent in the days of Shakespeare. It is now – with a few exceptions – neither powerful nor popular, and has become the pretty chambermaid to the lascivious. Nine-tenths of those who write for the theatre are gigolo dramatists in whom is no vestige of honour and scarcely a vestige of life. The stage is fully furnished now if it bears on its breast a bottle of champagne, a box of cigarettes, and a coyly covered bed. Not a bed for glorious love as in *Romeo and Juliet*, nor a bed for terrifying lust as in *Desire under the Elms*, but a bed for a mean and half-hearted pastime. The pomp and circumstance of life have been degraded down to the pomp and circumstance of a bed. Imagination has been lavished on the sheen of silk stockings and short chemises, too. There is a place, of course, for a pretty woman in a chemise and silk stockings in a play, but that place is not an important one, and a woman is something above and beyond a camisole. And the cult of these things has banished power and fantasy, music and song and greatness far from the drama, so that she is no longer a matron or maid, but a cheap, ageing and bedizened harlot.

We must go back for help and inspiration to the good and the great men. We must bring back to the drama its one-time simple austerity, its swinging merriment, its beauty in music of word and colour of scene, and its tragedy too deep for tears. Drama must be great, or at least fine, whether she has the lance in her breast or the crown on her head, whether she dons the simple serge of the religious or sports the coloured cap of folly.

An honoured English critic, [William Archer?] now safely housed in the grave, who wrote a few good things buried miles down in a lot of junk, said that passion and imitation constituted the elements of drama. Passion in primitive times was expressed, he goes on, not only by the voice, but by rhythmic movements of the body. Now the drama, he says, has grown out of dancing quite as much as out of song. Well, we're out to put dancing and song back again where they belong and make the movements of the body express something quite as well as the sound of the voice. When a man, says he, spoke in verse, he spoke as no man speaks in real life. This desire for real life on the stage has taken all the life out of the drama. The beauty, fire, and poetry of drama have perished in a storm of fake realisms. Let real birds fly through the air, real animals roam through the jungle, real fish swim in the sea, but let us have real art in the theatre.

And even in the most commonplace of realistic plays the symbol can never be absent. A house on a stage can never be a real house, and that which represents it must always be a symbol, be the scene ever so realistic. A room in a play, be it ever so realistic, must always remain a symbol for a room. There can never be any actuality on a stage, except an actuality that is absolutely unnecessary and utterly out of place. An actor representing a cavalier may come on stage mounted on a real horse, but the horse will always look ridiculous. The horse can have nothing to do with the drama. . . .

The closer we approach to actual life the further we move away from the drama. There is a deeper life than the life we see and hear with the open ear and the open eye, and this is the life important and the life everlasting. And this life can be caught from the group rather than from the individual. 'We can know a man only imperfectly,' says George Jean Nathan, in his *Intimate Notebooks*, 'for every man has an emotional, spiritual, philosophical and personal fourth dimension, of which no camera can catch a photograph.' So no dominant character in a play can give a full portrait of a man or a woman. Even Hamlet is not a picture of the whole man. Know a man all your life and you do not know him wholly, and how then can we expect to picture the nature of a man in the space of a couple of hours? True to life on the stage, as far as drama is concerned, really means true to death. So to hell with so-called realism, for it leads nowhere. . . .

Drama is tired of neat and trimly dressed plays that live their little day on the stage, stretch out their little hands for admiration and then sigh themselves down to the dead; plays that sprinkle us with scent instead of purging us with hyssop; that enthrone the sex force on a satin-sheeted bed in a room from which never issues the chant of unto us a child is born, unto us a son is given; plays whose high moments are movements with big bottles of champagne and little glasses of sherry; whose horizon of life is the regular ledges of a cocktail bar; whose ingenuity of technique consists of inventing obvious and commonplace excuses to get one character off the stage and bring another one in; plays in which the acting has become so refined that it has ceased to be acting at all; plays that have been dead a hundred years before they have been written. Poetry, passion, song, rhythm, rhetoric; exaggeration of emotion and gesture have been gutted out of the so-called modern drama; it has been purified out of existence. . . .

The new form in drama will take qualities found in classical, romantic, and expressionistic plays, will blend them together, breathe the breath of life into the new form and create a new drama. It will give rise to a new form of acting, a new form of production, a new response in the audience; authors, actors, and audience will be in communication with each other – three in one and one in three. If a play is what it ought to be it must be a religious function, whether it be played before a community of thousands or a community or ten. Gay, farcical, comic or tragical, it must be, not the commonplace portrayal of the trivial events in the life of this man or that woman, but a commentary of life itself. That is the main stream of great drama of the past. To achieve this, the veneration of realism, or, as Archer called it, pure imitation, must cease, and imagination be crowned queen of the drama again. . . .

New York Times, 21 Oct. 1934,
reprinted in *Blasts and Benedictions*, p. 111-17

The first thing I try to do is to make a play live: live as part of life, and live in its own right as a work of drama. Every character, every life, however minor, to have something to say comic or serious, and to say it well. Not an easy thing to do. These are the commonest things around us. We see them everywhere we go; see what they do, hear what they say; often laugh, sometimes wonder. But there are other parts, phases of life, and these, to my mind, should be prominent in the play. Above all, there is the imagination of man and that of the playwright; the comic, the serious and the poetical imagination; and, to my mind, these too should flash from any play worthy of an appearance on a stage; the comic imagination as in *The Frogs*; the sad imagination as in *The Dream Play*. Blake thought imagination to be the soul; Shaw thought it to be the Holy Ghost, and, perhaps, they weren't far out; for it is the most beautiful part of life whether it be on its knees in prayer or gallivanting about with a girl.

To me what is called naturalism, or even realism, isn't enough. They usually show life at its meanest and commonest, as if life never had time for a dance, a laugh, or a song. I always thought that life had a lot of time for these things, for each was a part of life itself; and so I broke away from realism into the chant of the second act of *The Silver Tassie*. But one scene in a play as a chant or a work of musical action and dialogue was not enough, so I set about trying to do this in an entire play, and brought forth *Cock-a-Doodle Dandy*. It is my favourite play; I think it is my best play – a personal opinion; the minds of others, linked with time, must decide whether I'm wrong or right.

The play is symbolical in more ways than one. The action manifests itself in Ireland, the mouths that speak are Irish mouths; but the spirit is to be found in action everywhere: the fight made by many to drive the joy of life from the hearts of men; the fight against this fight to vindicate the right of the joy of life courageously in the hearts of men. It isn't the clergy alone who booh and bluster against this joy of living, in dance, song, and story; . . . who interfere in the free flow of thought from man to man. Playwrights and poets have had, are having, a share in squeezing the mind of man into visions of woe and great lamentations. . . .

'O'Casey's Credo', *New York Times*, 9 Nov. 1958,
reprinted in *Playwrights on Playwriting*,
ed. Toby Cole (New York: Hill and Wang, 1960), p. 247-9,
and in *Blasts and Benedictions*, p. 142-5

I wasn't 'triggered off' in any particular way, or by any particular influence; that is, in playwriting. For better or worse, I am a blend of experience and absorption of the spirit in the old, old melodrama, which you never saw; of Shakespeare, and the Elizabethans; of Goldsmith, Sheridan, Shaw; with the insistent influence of the romantic poets, and of everything I read, including the Americans: Whitman, Jefferson, Emerson, Melville, Hawthorne, and Lincoln. In fact: a world of life is within me, and, I suppose, I have moulded it all into an O'Casey figure of colour, line, form. . . .

By the way, like Shaw, I was born a Communist, and have been one all my life. I was one long before I heard the name of Lenin, as was G.B.S.; and as a born Communist I am intensely interested in all phases of life, from the lilies of the field up to the stars in the sky.

Letter to Ronald Gene Rollins, 25 July 1959, printed in his
Sean O'Casey's Drama: Verisimilitude and Vision, p. 115

a: Primary Sources

Publication details of individual plays are included in Section 1, and of autobiographies, collected letters, and miscellaneous prose in Section 3.

Collections of Plays

Five Irish Plays. London: Macmillan, 1935. [*Juno and the Paycock*, *The Shadow of a Gunman*, *The Plough and the Stars*, *The End of the Beginning*, *A Pound on Demand*.]

Collected Plays I. London: Macmillan, 1949. [*Juno and the Paycock*, *The Shadow of a Gunman*, *The Plough and the Stars*, *The End of the Beginning*, *A Pound on Demand*.]

Collected Plays II. London: Macmillan, 1949. [*The Silver Tassie*, *Within the Gates*, *The Star Turns Red*, all in the revised versions.]

Collected Plays III. London: Macmillan, 1951. [*Purple Dust*, *Red Roses for Me*, *Hall of Healing*: first publication of one-act play, with minor revisions to others.]

Collected Plays IV. London: Macmillan, 1951. [*Oak Leaves and Lavender*, *Cock-a-Doodle Dandy*, *Bedtime Story*, *Time to Go*: first publication of the one-act plays.]

Selected Plays. New York: George Braziller, 1954. [*The Shadow of the Gunman*, *Juno and the Paycock*, *The Plough and the Stars*, *The Silver Tassie*, *Within the Gates*, *Purple Dust*, *Red Roses for Me*, *Bedtime Story*, *Time to Go*.]

Three Plays. London: Macmillan, 1957, and 1966; Pan Books, 1980. [*Juno and the Paycock*, *The Shadow of a Gunman*, *The Plough and the Stars*.]

Five One-Act Plays. London: Macmillan, 1958, and 1966. [*The End of the Beginning*, *A Pound on Demand*, *Hall of Healing*, *Bedtime Story*, *Time to Go*.]

Three More Plays, with an introduction by J.C. Trewin. London: Macmillan, 1965 and 1969. [*The Silver Tassie*, *Purple Dust*, *Red Roses for Me*: final revised version of latter play.]

Six Plays. Pennsylvania: Franklin, 1980. [*Juno and the Paycock, The Plough and the Stars, Purple Dust, Red Roses for Me, Oak Leaves and Lavender, The Bishop's Bonfire*.]

The Complete Plays of Sean O'Casey 1. London: Macmillan, 1984. [*Juno and the Paycock, The Shadow of a Gunman, The Plough and the Stars, The End of the Beginning, A Pound on Demand*.]

The Complete Plays of Sean O'Casey 2. London: Macmillan, 1984. [*The Silver Tassie, Within the Gates, The Star Turns Red*.]

The Complete Plays of Sean O'Casey 3. London: Macmillan, 1984. [*Purple Dust, Red Roses for Me, Hall of Healing*.]

The Complete Plays of Sean O'Casey 4. London: Macmillan, 1984. [*Oak Leaves and Lavender, Cock-a-Doodle Dandy, Bedtime Story, Time to Go*.]

The Complete Plays of Sean O'Casey 5. London: Macmillan, 1984. [*The Bishop's Bonfire, The Drums of Father Ned, Behind the Green Curtains, Figuro in the Night, The Moon Shines on Kylenamoe, The Harvest Festival, Kathleen Listens In, Nannie's Night Out*.]

Contributions to Radio and Television

The Playwright and the Box Office. BBC, 25 June 1938. [Discussion between O'Casey and Maurice Browne. The text was printed in *The Listener*, 7 July 1938, and reprinted in *Blasts and Benedictions*, p. 3-8.]

Sean O'Casey Talks. Radio Eireann, 15, 22, 29 May 1955. ['The playwright looks at the Ireland of his plays and at the Ireland of To-day.']

A Conversation with Sean O'Casey. NBC-TV, 22 Jan. 1956. [Discussion between O'Casey and Robert Emmett Ginna, filmed at the author's home in Torquay, Devon. Released as a documentary film by Encyclopaedia Britannica Films, 1958.]

The Exile. BBC1-TV, 6 Feb. 1968. [Filmed study of O'Casey, directed by Don Taylor, in the *Omnibus* series.]

A Celebration of Sean O'Casey. BBC2-TV, 30 Mar. 1980. [Biographical portrait and critical assessment written by Andy O'Mahony and produced by Robin Wylie for BBC Northern Ireland.]

Films

Cradle of Genius. Plough Productions, Dublin, 1969, released in
 USA by Irving Lester Enterprises, 1961. [Film about the
 Abbey Theatre, directed by Paul Rotha, including a
 conversation between O'Casey and Barry Fitzgerald.]
Young Cassidy. Sextant Films, London, 1965, released in USA
 by MGM. [Screenplay by John Whiting, based loosely on
 parts of *Mirror in My House*, dealing with O'Casey's early
 years, dir. Jack Cardiff, with Rod Taylor in the title role.]

Records

Sean O'Casey Reading from His Works. Caedmon TC 1012,
 CDL 51012 (cassette). [Including extracts from *Juno and the
 Paycock*, *Inishfallen Fare Thee Well*, and *Pictures in the
 Hallway*, recorded at O'Casey's home in Totnes, Devon,
 12 Nov. 1952, and released 1953.]
Sean O'Casey Reading, Volume Two. Caedmon TC 1198, CDL
 51198 (cassette). [Including extracts from *I Knock at the
 Door*, *Rose and Crown*, and *Sunset and Evening Star*, with
 'The Wearing of the Green', traditional song sung by
 O'Casey, recorded at O'Casey's home in Totnes, Devon,
 26 Dec. 1953, and released 1969.]
Sean O'Casey's World. Center for Cassette Studies, 010-3107.
 [Sound track of television programme 'A Conversation with
 Sean O'Casey and Robert Emmett Ginna', NBC-TV, 22 Jan.
 1956, released 1970.]
The Green Crow Caws: Sean O'Casey. EMI Records, EMA
 793. [Poems, songs, and prose performed by John Kevanagh,
 dir. Sean Murphy, released 1980.]

b: Secondary Sources

Theatrical and Social Background

Una Ellis-Fermor, *The Irish Dramatic Movement*. London:
 Methuen, 1939; reprinted 1967.
Lady Gregory's Journals, ed. Lennox Robinson. London:
 Putman, 1946.

Joseph Holloway's Abbey Theatre, ed. Robert Hogan and
    Michael J. O'Neill. Carbondale: Southern Illinois University
    Press, 1967. [Selection from his unpublished journal.]
Michael O hAodha, *Theatre in Ireland*. Oxford: Blackwell,
    1974.
Katharine Worth, *The Irish Drama in Europe from Yeats to
    Beckett*. London: Athlone Press, 1978.
Hugh Hunt, *The Abbey, Ireland's National Theatre 1904-1979*.
    Dublin: Gill and Macmillan, 1979.
Christopher Fitz-Simon, *The Irish Theatre*. London: Thames and
    Hudson, 1983.

Journal

The Sean O'Casey Review, an international journal of O'Casey
    studies, ed. Robert G. Lowery, Holbrook, New York. Volume
    I (1974) – Volume VIII (1982). [Essays and articles by
    O'Casey scholars, theatre practitioners etc.; regular reviews of
    books and productions; ephemera.]

Selected Critical Articles and Books

J. Koslow, *The Green and the Red: Sean O'Casey, the Man and
    his Plays*. New York: Golden Griffen Books, 1950, reprinted
    in revised and expanded edition as *Sean O'Casey: the Man
    and His Plays* (New York: Citadel, 1966).
David Krause, *Sean O'Casey: the Man and His Work*. London:
    McGibbon and Kee, 1960. [The first comprehensive study of
    O'Casey's life and works with extensive notes including
    background material and bibliographical references; excellent
    overall introduction to the playwright.]
Robert Hogan, *The Experiments of Sean O'Casey*. New York: St
    Martin's Press, 1960. [Examination of O'Casey's dramatic
    method, the innovations and experiments in form, including
    the later plays. Detailed documentation of *The Silver Tassie*
    controversy as an appendix.]
Saros Cowasjee, *Sean O'Casey: the Man behind the Plays*.
    Edinburgh: Oliver and Boyd, 1963.
Gabriel Fallon, *Sean O'Casey: the Man I Knew*. London:
    Routledge, 1965. [Critical account of O'Casey based on
    personal reminiscences by the author; their close friendship
    ended after many years when Fallon, an actor turned drama

critic, was less than sympathetic to O'Casey's later plays.]

Sean McCann, ed., *The World of Sean O'Casey*. London: Four Square Books, 1966. [The book is divided into three sections: ten short biographical essays; a collection of anecdotes; and five essays on the plays, the autobiographies, and the letters.]

William A. Armstrong, *Sean O'Casey* (Writers and Their Work). London: Longman, 1967. [Brief survey with select bibliography.]

David Krause, *A Self-Portrait of the Artist as a Man: Sean O'Casey's Letters*. Dublin: Dolmen Press, 1968. [View of O'Casey 'as it emerges from his extensive correspondence over many years'.]

Ronald Ayling, ed., *Sean O'Casey* (Modern Judgements). London: Macmillan, 1969. [With a notable introduction by the editor, this is a well balanced selection of essays, together with reviews of early London productions.]

Martin B. Margulies, *The Early Life of Sean O'Casey*. Dublin: Dolmen Press, 1970. [Deals interestingly with O'Casey's life up to 1920.]

Bernard Benstock, *Sean O'Casey* (Irish Writers). Lewisburg: Bucknell University Press, 1970. [Monograph which includes an analysis of all O'Casey's major plays, discussion of the autobiographies, and an examination of how settings and stage directions add to the impact of selected plays.]

Maureen Malone, *The Plays of Sean O'Casey*. Carbondale: Southern Illinois University Press, 1970. [Social, economic, political, and religious backgrounds to the plays.]

Eileen O'Casey, *Sean*. London: Macmillan, 1971. [Moving biography by his wife, from their meeting in London in 1926.]

Herbert Goldstone, *In Search of Community: the Achievement of Sean O'Casey*. Dublin: Mercier Press, 1972. [Commitment and community in O'Casey's work, with analysis and evaluation of the plays.]

E.H. Mikhail and John O'Riordan, eds., *The Sting and the Twinkle: Conversations with Sean O'Casey*. London: Macmillan, 1974. [Interviews and recollections from actors, directors, theatre critics and journalists.]

Thomas Kilroy, ed., *Sean O'Casey* (Twentieth Century Views). New Jersey: Prentice-Hall, 1975. [Collection of essays including one previously unpublished by John Arden and a review of *Windfalls* by Samuel Beckett.]

Doris da Rin, *Sean O'Casey* (World Dramatists). New York: Ungar, 1976. [The discussions of the plays are largely plot summaries with little critical evaluation.]